SLAMMED

Overcoming Tragedy in the Wave of Grief

ANDREA MAHER

55:11
PUBLISHING

ACKNOWLEDGEMENTS

This book would not have been possible if not for the relentless and sweet nagging of a dear friend Kristie Shackelford, who set the entire process in motion by believing strongly in her heart that others would benefit when "slammed" with their own personal tragedy.

I would also like to thank my editor and dear friend Cherri Olsen, who has been by my side through all of my major ups and downs as a close friend and sister in Christ. I am indebted to her for putting her brilliant mind and superior editing abilities to my writing throughout the years, always making me look the better for it.

To my sister Dee, who possesses the compassionate heart of King David: You have walked with me every step of the way, and in many cases supernaturally taken on my pain and burden. Your selfless personality and empathetic nature came to my rescue more times than I could ever thank you. The endless tears that you had to endure and the conversations we shared will forever be cherished in my heart. *"Two are better than one, because they have a good return for their labor. If either of them falls down, one can help the other up. But pity anyone who falls and has no one to help them up"* (Ecclesiastes 4:9-10). You have picked me up more than a lifetime's worth.

There would be no story without my beloved gifts, my children: John, Anthony, Michael, and Matthew. You have brought many smiles to my face as well as many tears from my heart. I love and miss you, my son John, from the depths of my heart, and I look forward to our reunion in Heaven one day. I am thankful to God for leaving a piece of you here on earth in your precious daughter, Alivia. And Matthew, your example after your "great fall" is an inspiration to me in that you have clearly shown that the measure of a man is not whether he falls, but how he gets up after a fall.

For my ever-supportive husband, John, who has walked by my side for over 40 years and has been my earthly rock: You have displayed godly leadership in our family in all ways. I am beyond grateful for your continual encouragement, for making me feel so valued when everything around me seemed to indicate the contrary. Thank you for reminding me of the God we serve and His sovereign hand in our lives.

Thank You to my Lord and Savior Jesus Christ who has carried me when I didn't think I could take another step. My Father in Heaven Who is always faithful, always full of grace, always intimate; Who is alive and well, working actively in the lives of His children in this present day and age.

CONTENTS

PREFACE

I was an impressionable young girl. I would watch a scary movie and then look over my shoulder for months, certain there were boogiemen under my bed and intruders behind the shower curtain. I was hooked on *The Twilight Zone*, an American anthology TV series created and narrated by Rod Serling. The show was a suspenseful drama, with stories that focused on paranormal and disturbing events. I remember huddling on the sofa with my older sister, Denise ("Dee"), sneaking in yet another frightful episode. We were both under the age of 10, and the rushing adrenaline of anticipation rendered us silent and immobile as we waited for the plot to unfold. A group of doctors stood facing their patient, her eyes wrapped tightly with bandages and gauze. They were about to remove the bandages, and the patient—along with two very freaked-out little girls—were about to see for the first time the grossly distorted pig-faces of the aliens staring down at her.

Like tightly wound coils suddenly released, my sister and I sprang off the sofa simultaneously, shrieking as we made our way for the staircase. We were fighting for our lives, and we roughly shoved one another back down the stairs as we climbed to safety. Just behind our heels, we were certain, was the grasp of a creature ready to claw at our feet. Our grandmother had been sleeping upstairs, and her unexpected appearance in the hallway sparked another set of panicked screams as we collided with her in the doorway. Gramma's groggy, "What'sa matta?" quickly shifted from concern to frenzied Italian fury as she realized there was no brutal attack under-way, but simply two granddaughters terrorized by a show they never should have been watching in the first place.

We were too cowed to stick around in Gramma's room and too scared to go back down and turn off the television, so we made a break for the guest room and spent the rest of the night taking turns sleeping and keeping watch for imminent danger. That was the last time I was invited to sleep at Gramma's.

Then there was Alfred Hitchcock's timeless thriller, *Psycho*, where the beautiful blonde gets stabbed to death in the shower by the wacky voyeur, Norman Bates. I am still haunted by that scene every time I'm alone in a hotel room.

These vicarious experiences stayed with me into adulthood and framed who I am and how I think. Shocking and traumatic events deliver an impact, and we are changed by them whether we realize it or not.

I grew up at the seashore. I know the helpless feel-ing that comes with being tricked and tumbled by a brutal wave. One moment I am standing on my feet; a moment later, I am relentlessly tossed and pounded by a force too powerful to defy. It's the epitome of loss of control.

Unfortunately, the following scenario visits me often, courtesy of a recurring dream likely borne from a blend of past scary stories, real-life traumas, and a large dose of my own overactive imagination. The dream always begins on a beach. I am swimming and floating in the water in perfect peace; then off in the distance, I notice a break in the calm—an unexpected shift in the wind. The current changes abruptly, the jostling waves feel unnatural, and the darkening atmosphere is ominously quiet. An eruption in the deep has unveiled a towering, monstrous wall of water heading straight for the coast—bearing down on me. I stare helplessly at the rising ocean as those around me carry on as usual, blissfully unaware of the oncoming disaster.

I turn and attempt to run through the water, arms flailing and legs straining to gain momentum against the weight of the water. I look around to see others systematically swept under by the torrent, and I am certain it is only a matter of time before it gets me, too. I try to swim faster, push harder, but my feet barely move. I feel heavy, out of control, and terrified. My suffocating demise is only moments away, when a jolt snatches me from my horror and there I am—with pounding heart and streaming night sweats, I kick off the covers and frantically rub my eyes until the blinking red numbers of the digital alarm clock on the bedside table come into view. If I had stayed asleep, the wave would surely have buried me alive. I would not have lived to see the new dawn.

Little did I know that on December 15, 2005, this nightmare would invade my wakeful life, and I would find myself in the throes of a ruthless tidal wave of horror in broad daylight. This time there was no reassuring return from the netherworld of dreams to the real world of consciousness. This wasn't "only a dream," and I wouldn't be rubbing my eyes to behold digital numbers marking their steady, familiar tempo. There would be no relief.

I had been slammed—snatched from my peaceful stride and hurled into the undercurrent of tragedy. The tsunami had reached me, enveloped me, consumed me, and flung me mercilessly. I had become as insubstantial as a rag doll. I had been slammed, knocked out, pulled under, shaken, and rearranged so haphazardly that I found myself paralyzed—unable to move and with no clue what I should do next. My worst fear had outrun me, had outsmarted me, and had infiltrated my security—replacing my faith with fury and my expectations with mighty letdowns.

I had never been here before. This wasn't my world. This wasn't my life. I didn't belong here—floundering in this danger zone. I was tumbling, drowning, and painfully aware that I would have to muster every ounce of strength if I wanted to stay afloat.

But I didn't want to float. Not anymore. I wanted to surrender to the water and follow the currents down, down, down. I wanted to breathe in the heaviness and allow the weight of my sorrow to crush any shred of survival left in me. For the first time, I pleaded with my reality—begging and bargaining for the mercy of sleep. This time, I wanted to close my eyes and never wake up.

Maybe you have been slammed by some life-shattering event. How could your outlook suddenly become this sad and dismal? How will you cope? What will you do? How can you bear up under this burden? How can you face the fear? How can you go on? Staying asleep seems better than waking up to face the pain all over again.

I know. I've been slammed. More than once.

I can identify with the helpless confusion surrounding a tragedy, a heartbreaking loss, a failure. The only sounds that reach your ears are the bellowing cries incited by the catastrophe. Obsessive thoughts hammer you, punctuated by unanswered questions and endless speculation. No matter how many times you revisit the situation, you cannot make sense of it. Like a misplaced puzzle piece, it just doesn't fit. It will never fit—because in your mind and wildest imaginings, your life wasn't supposed to turn out this way.

Of course, life is a series of trials and tribulations. Many are serious difficulties, and they can weigh us down—make us disengage from "normal" life for a while. But there are some experiences that are so unforeseen, so outside our scope of rational assumptions and predictions that we find ourselves slammed—staring and stalling, barely breathing, as we shuffle through each baffling day while we wonder despairingly about what could have been and what should have been.

Although our stories vary, our pain feels exactly the same; and each one of us is expected to cope, to get better, to go on … but how?

I don't claim to have the magical answers. I simply have my story and a growing collection of *life preservers* that were pitched my way at various points in my struggle. Such as the words of one perceptive woman, who whispered to me during an otherwise festive event shortly after tragedy struck my family: "You won't always feel this way, I promise." She had been slammed by a similar tragedy years earlier so the life preserver she sent to me came with the knowledge of her own experience. Or the time a doctor explained that the physical manifestations of grief are comparable to those suffered in a major car accident.

Some helped, some didn't, and others I clung to as though my very life depended on it. Take what helps you, throw away what doesn't, and—most importantly—believe that there will be better days ahead. Right now you can't see it. Right now you'd prefer to sleep or surrender to the current, but time has a way of bringing healing and understanding from the chaos and pain.

I pray my journey will encourage you to hang on in the wake of the storm that threatens to destroy your spirit. I won't dwell on the many heart-wrenching subplots, but I will share the most poignant lessons I've learned along the way. This is my own personal survival guide that kept me floating when I wanted to surrender to the weight of my circumstances. I do not overvalue my experience nor do I trivialize anyone else's. Pain is pain is pain. The question is: *How will you live with it?*

CHAPTER ONE

CALM BEFORE THE STORM

It was early evening, and my oldest son, still affectionately called Little John at age 28 and standing at 6 feet, seemed agitated as he left the bathroom. With a jagged sidestep he evaded me, leaving me standing in the hallway to watch his shirtless silhouette disappear around the corner.

I stumbled as I hurried to make the phone call. My husband, a career officer in law enforcement, was teaching at the police academy; he would know what to do. My husband always knew what to do. He was strong, levelheaded, and capable of finding the balanced perspective in the midst of erratic chaos and uncertainty. "It is what it is," was his trademark response to incidents that would throw me into a panic. He would always redirect the fruitless expending of my energy to focusing on God's faithfulness and the bigger picture.

My mind raced to recall our hallway conversation. Little John had been in the bathroom so long, and his eyes looked weird. I had confronted him. "Are you using again?"

There was no answer, just a quick bounce from his high-school basketball days and he was past me. I stared at the back of his head as he made his way to the other side of our home. I raced upstairs, out of earshot, to call my husband. John Sr. answered the phone and seemed short, abrupt, distracted. *Why wasn't he getting it?*

Danger was brewing, my control was slipping, and our son could likely be back in hiding by tomorrow morning. Little John's reflexive reaction to conflict was mirrored in our hallway meeting. He would always avoid or withdraw—escape to his world of solitude until he was doing well again or until the furor had subsided. He was predictable in many ways, and isolation was likely his next move.

I dreaded those times of disappearing. Why did Little John bolt when he was slipping? Did his father and I make him feel that he had no other choice? Was it something I said or did? Every once in a while I would allow my mind to wrestle with the genesis of this pattern and what role we played in the process. Were our standards too high? Were we so judgmental that he preferred loneliness? I never wanted to be unapproachable. Neither did I want to be an enabler. Part of me felt validated by Little John's vanishing act—a tinge of satisfaction in his tendency to shy away when he was in the throes of his addictions, as if it somehow indicated he knew better.

Even so, the times when Little John would disappear were suffused with heaviness. My unsettled heart could not be soothed while my child was suffering and our communication was severed. His periodic retreats brought the sad contradiction of peace in our physical home while turmoil stirred within our souls. Those periods were hard for me because he stayed away for days at a time, maintaining silence; and upon his eventual return, he would never look me in the eye.

I was still on the phone with John, when I suddenly heard the car start up. *Was that a car I just heard?* I could've sworn a car was pulling out of our driveway, but that wasn't possible. I ran back down the steps, my husband still on the line.

I peered out the side window panel of the front door and could see Little John turned halfway around in the driver's seat as he backed the car down the driveway and out onto the road. I stayed at the window to see if he might look in my direction, allowing me to communicate a truce or try to gauge his mood. He never turned his head as he sped off down the road, so I reluctantly returned my attention to my husband, who was still on the line and waiting patiently—as usual.

"He didn't even have a shirt on!" I argued, to no one in particular. My husband asked me to clarify, but there was no time for that. Instead, I told him to come home quickly, and he promised to look for Little John on his way—check our son's usual retreats. I tried to replay our hallway conversation, imbued with my suspicions about Little John's drug use. He had emerged from the bathroom shirtless, so I thought I had more time—at least enough time to go upstairs and make a phone call. But the next thing I knew, he was gone.

Ever since I can remember, I had an idealistic vision of what my life was going to look like. I married the person I fell in love with when I was in high school and he was in college. By the time I was Little John's age, 28, I was the proud and eager mother of John Jr., Anthony, Michael, and Matthew.

Parenthood infused our home with unpredictability—a characteristic I would never intentionally seek or schedule into my meticulously well-managed life. God gave me four boys—competitive, athletic, and saturated with testosterone. All four were bent on shaking up my careful stability with their reptilian pets, wrestling matches, muddy shoes, and grass-stained clothes. Into my immaculate house, they brought soaring soccer balls and an endless parade of cousins and neighbor kids. Our home became the base for church, school, and sports activities—all seamlessly organized on my color-coded calendar. I had this down, this mothering thing, and I planned to run this ship with every resource I had to offer.

My mind would lazily drift to the future from time to time, and in my mind's eye I wished my four boys well as they obediently marched out our front door and into their lives of guaranteed success. I watched as they drove off into the sunset—standing at the door with beaming face, surrounded by the comforting aromas of bleach and simmering garlic. My four godly men of integrity would one day leave our nest with every benefit we could possibly give them. Surely God would use them in a mighty way to impact their generation, and their legacy would continue for generations to come!

With that idealistic vision in mind, I proceeded to do everything in my power to nurture those four boys. I was a stay-at-home mom who taught them to read prior to kindergarten, volunteered in their classrooms, coached their teams, and taught their Sunday school classes and church clubs. I monitored their daily activities and routines like a true Italian mama should. Cleanliness, order, structure, discipline—I was determined to create a home life full of love, playfulness, conversation, and competition. I scheduled time for everything: homework, Bible study, reading time, playtime, TV time, etc. Routine and structure were my mantras. Surely controlling every minute of every day would guarantee well-adjusted, disciplined kids who would grow up to be secure, smart, brave, self-assured leaders in their world—men who could withstand all forms of evil.

My faith journey began in an Irish-Italian Roman Catholic home where, in my 20s, I moved from practicing the organized religion of my youth to a personal relationship with Jesus Christ. Accepting Jesus as my Savior filled that spiritual void in my life and confirmed that my life would continue on schedule, just like I planned it. I was a Christian now, living for God and teaching my children to do the same so there were only good things on my horizon.

What is a strong, healthy family? I could tell you, because I kept a running list in my head and proudly checked each box as I methodically reviewed our performance as parents. *God. Church. Strong marriage. Healthy balance of love and discipline. Community involvement.* All boxes were checked, and therefore all indicators that the rewards for our labor would be waiting just around the corner.

I enjoyed going to church, attending Bible study, and learning more about my newfound faith in a personal God. I plunged into church life like I did everything else: feet first. I led in a variety of ways. Life as a Christian couldn't be better. I was happy, with the Lord by my side. All was indeed good.

As the boys got older, commitments got bigger and busyness overshadowed our lives. The boys excelled in sports and academics, and each one cheered and challenged the other brothers. The younger siblings had the added advantage of their older brothers' reputations preceding them, which insured instantaneous acceptance into their peer groups and an immediate spotlight on their athletic prowess. The boys confidently involved themselves in every aspect of their young lives, from extracurricular activities to sports to academics. My husband and I didn't miss one bit of it.

They all served as captains of their teams. During their sports seasons, I couldn't wait to get up for the morning newspaper because I knew that I would see their names in the box scores. Frequently, they were headliners.

When Little John hit his senior year in high school, life took a turn for all of us. He started to slowly veer off. He was hanging with the wrong crowd and was soon cutting school. My smooth-sailing life became unexpectedly rocky. John was still involved in sports, but his grades were slipping.

After 17 years of seemingly successful navigation, I was about to venture into uncharted territory. I did not understand my son or his choices. Arguments ensued; the tension created an unfamiliar gap between him and me, which threw me off-center. I was no longer in control, and this uncharacteristic status made me feel weak.

This challenging time—with all the feelings of helplessness, fear, anger, and frustration—prompted me to re-evaluate my own walk with God. Where was my so-called strong faith during this, my first real crisis? It was during that shaky time that the Word of God truly became new and fresh to me. I began to read the Scriptures with a voracious hunger for answers. With renewed eyes accompanied by a sad and heavy heart, I began to see all the examples of biblical characters—real people of their day—dealing with failures and uncertainties; I saw how reliance on God made all the difference in their journey.

I yearned for a way to reach my son, to resolve the problems at hand, to cope with my helpless fear of watching him adopt a lifestyle that promised to destroy him. I had a zillion thoughts swirling in my mind constantly, and it was then that I realized I needed to reverse my seating position of the last 17 years. I had cheerfully and confidently placed myself in the captain's seat of my life, accepting Jesus as my co-pilot—whom I consulted when I needed him, and until that point I hadn't. Since I suddenly had no idea where I was going in these strange waters, I knew I needed to switch seats—and do so as quickly as possible. Loss of control and threatening storms had me making a much-needed course correction. My only solution at hand was to throw myself on the mercy of God and ask Him to take over.

It was evident that our son had started smoking pot. His attitude became increasingly apathetic. He seemed to wander aimlessly through his days, and his lack of motivation was the focus of many failed attempts at conversations with him—and the cause of many sleepless nights for me. With nowhere to look for help but upward, I desperately prayed for stability, for spiritual footing that would strengthen me as I tried to cope with his fluctuating moods and behaviors. One day I heard a particular sermon on a Christian radio station that challenged my prayer life, and I was willing to try anything. So I began a serious prayer regimen—a time alone with God while I pleaded, cried, and entreated Him for a solution on behalf of Little John. God had my undivided attention now.

My exercise in prayer shifted from a bland, sporadic, and vacuous ritual to an action of purpose and intent. I prayed to God on my knees. This was a major turning point in my life as my relationship with God evolved into a deeper, more intimate relationship. I poured out my heart and soul in ways I couldn't do with anyone else.

For John's three younger brothers, life went on relatively undisturbed; however, my perspective had changed. Although achievement was still ranked high, my view was more balanced. My disappointed heart produced a much-needed shuffling of priorities, and suddenly achievement wasn't at the top of the list anymore. God was tweaking my vision to be more in line with His, and my vise-grip of control had loosened. The metamorphosis was painful, and I still fought to keep control as I grappled with the emotions that went along with the daily torture of loving a child determined to walk a path of destruction.

There is a saying that a mother's heart is only as peaceful as her most struggling child, and I would attest that this is true. The 10-year battle for my son sent my heart to unfamiliar depths and tainted the joys with shadows of angst and dread. Everything was right, but nothing was right because the underlying subject of addiction was always present—permeating all other topics with uncertainty and fear. My perspective needed constant readjusting, but my faith and reliance on the Lord was growing. I stayed close to Him in each valley and through each storm.

In the fall, following his high-school graduation, we dropped John off at college, hoping this was exactly what he needed to head in a new direction. John had always been intelligent, perceptive, and stoic. He had always relished the solitary enjoyment of reading. These qualities combined with the independence of living on his own in an academic environment with a new crowd of focused and success-minded peers seemed promising to us, his parents. We prayed this would be the answer for his future.

The day the notice arrived from the college, my embattled heart once again plummeted as I took in the news that John could not return for the second semester after failing every course. His decision to trade his books and future degree for a risky lifestyle was revolting to me. This was the death of a dream, the death of *my* dream—the first of many dashed hopes for my oldest son. From this time on, the emotional temperature in our household would have more ups and downs than a well-oiled seesaw.

Over the next decade, John moved in and out of our home numerous times. He held countless jobs, each one briefly. He checked himself into rehab facilities with faith-based, Christ-centered programs on two separate occasions; each time he emerged stronger, more committed to the Lord and clean living. And each time our hopes rose and fell as we watched him battle depression, withdrawal, and the ever-present temptation to fall back down the slippery slope of drug addiction.

John's struggles took their toll on the dynamics of our entire family. Those years were characterized by my own war with taking, and letting go of, control. The work, the worry, and the strain were overpowering at times and created turbulence in our household. But all the while, this trial with John was changing me and bringing me closer to God.

John moved away to Philadelphia at the age of 20. Although I wasn't sure how he was doing on a day-to-day basis, I relished the calm that returned to my house. No more sleepless nights spent waiting to hear his key in the door indicating that he was finally home from wherever he had been, doing whatever he felt like doing at any particular time. After he left, I committed to writing and calling him regularly. I prayed this separation from his old friends and familiar habits would be the catalyst for a new life and new beginning. I was glad he was finally away from the classic small-town mentality with all its narrowness and pitfalls. The never-ending party scene, the connections he had established, and the reputation he had developed were no match for the best of his intentions. That year in a new city will be forever marked in my memory as "the best of years; the worst of years"—a dichotomy once described by Dickens.

In the midst of the precariousness of John's world in Philadelphia, so many wonderful things were happening on our peaceful home front. Anthony continued to excel in soccer and had accepted a full athletic scholarship to college. Michael was at the top of his class and applying to the United States Naval Academy. Matthew was playing on the Olympic Development Team for soccer and seemed to be advancing far more quickly in sports than any of his brothers had before him. My husband was appointed chief of police, and I had just been awarded a federal grant to teach abstinence education in the public schools. To top it off, my years of writing the freelance column "Family Matters" led to an offer from the publisher of our county newspaper to oversee the creation and launch of his company's new magazine, *Parent ABCs*, in the leading role of editor-in-chief.

That spring, we were finally able to afford our first family vacation. Prior vacations had entailed packing the kids in the van and driving over 1,000 miles to stay with my parents in their adults-only community in Florida. Within 20 minutes of our arrival, the senior citizens' patrol would show up, responding to a report of a soccer ball stuck in a palm tree. At the clubhouse, my four overactive boys were met with stony stares and snide comments because they had walked in without shoes on their feet. This was not a fun family get-away, but it had been all we could afford. So I could not have been more excited, anticipating our first real vacation at a hotel.

The evening before we left, I listened to a powerful sermon on the importance of giving up our kids completely to the will and plan of God. I thought I had done that already, but by the end of this radio message I realized I was afraid to do it. The speaker challenged me: "Have you ever said, 'Lord, do whatever you need to with my child'?"

As I listened intently, my mind swirled with arguments: *"That is fine if your kids are doing well, but try saying that if you have a wayward child involved in risky behaviors."* Nevertheless, I felt inclined to exercise my faith. After all, I was feeling good about everything else going on in our lives, so it made sense to show God that I did indeed trust Him with my children. Right then and there, I got on my knees and prayed in all sincerity, "Lord, do whatever you need to do to get John's attention; but, Lord, please don't do it in our county."

We left for Florida. Three days later, while enjoying the best time of our lives, my husband received a call from the captain of his police department. The captain had bad news. Our son John had been arrested for selling drugs—in our county; and not just in our county, but in his father's jurisdiction as the newly named chief of police. *SLAMMED!*

If I thought John's failure in college brought a shock to my world, this devastation was no comparison. My body was paralyzed and my mind shattered by the shame of being the parent of a child who had broken the law. Absolute disdain, resentment, and anger swelled up inside me against my son. Little John had destroyed his future, and in the process he had humiliated his parents and tarnished our reputations. John and I were notable public figures, and this was a very public disgrace.

Only minutes before that fateful phone call, I was feeling celebratory as we prepared to head off to Disney World to watch the fireworks. Our lives seemed secure in so many ways. Moments later, I was cast down into the depths of shame and hopelessness.

> VOICE OF TRUTH: LIKE THE TIDES, LIFE IS FILLED WITH EBBS AND FLOWS. NEVER GET TOO HIGH ON THE MOUNTAIN OR TOO LOW IN THE VALLEY, AND LEARN TO SAY, "IN WHATEVER SITUATION I AM IN, I WILL BE CONTENT."

I took this news hard, and it was only the beginning. The following years would be marked by suspicion, distrust, embarrassment, and upsetting interactions with the court system. I didn't want to return home and face the scrutiny or the media press that surrounded the arrest: "New Police Chief's Son Arrested for Dealing Drugs." I felt the irony of those earlier mornings when I loved getting up to read the headlines with my child's name featured prominently.

I continued to learn a lot about my prideful heart. I didn't want to continue writing my column—a platform I had used to address policies that favored the traditional family. In losing face, I felt I had lost my voice. One day the phone rang with a call from the publisher's wife. She encouraged me, saying I would now be a better writer because all people have problems; this incident will make my "perfect" family more real and relatable. It was the encouragement I needed to keep writing—and reveal the painful truth of the journey.

This ordeal taught me more about myself than about my son. In the eyes of my Heavenly Father, I was no different from my son. You may not find me dabbling in unlawful activities, but what about my self-righteous attitude—what about my pride? These activities are unlawful in God's kingdom. They are sins that God recognizes as surely as everyone else could recognize my son's wrongdoing. It became obvious that God was not only at work on John's life, but He was retooling my heart as well.

I shared these new realizations with Little John. I wanted him to know that God still loved me no matter what; likewise, we loved and supported him no matter what. Life never got easier for either of us, but my relationship with God got stronger as I learned to fight my battles on my knees. Through prayer, I coped.

The Christmas season of 2004 brought new announcements and changes for our family. My husband retired as chief of police and assumed a new position as executive undersheriff for Cape May County. All four boys—now men—were home for the holidays. Little John was living at home again, holding down a job, and doing the best he had in years. Anthony had graduated from Mercyhurst College in Erie, Pa., and was residing in Kansas City, playing professional soccer for the Comets. Mike was a senior at the Naval Academy. Matt was a sophomore at Temple University.

After Christmas brunch, John and Anthony came into the kitchen and approached their father and me. They wanted to speak with us, they said. My heart instantly flew into a forceful reverberation, hammering against the confines of my rib cage—I knew the four brothers had been out and about the town the night before. Anthony began by quoting a familiar Bible verse. "You know, Mom, 'children are a gift from the Lord and the fruit of the womb is His reward.'"

My expression remained blank as I strove to comprehend his meaning. It was at that moment that Anthony announced, on behalf of his brother, that John was going to be a father. His girlfriend, Mary Kate, was pregnant. While I was thrown off by this unexpected news, I felt a tiny bubble of hope rise deep within me once again. *This might be the very thing to keep John on the straight and narrow for the rest of his adult life.* He had been doing so well the past two years—working a steady job, staying clean from drugs. I pondered the possibility that being a daddy would solidify his goals and work ethic.

I had taught my children (and innumerable other children through the public schools and churches) that sex was reserved for marriage. And later that night, my dreams were filled with doubts and fears for surely my public persona as an abstinence educator would once again be mocked and come under attack for having a grandchild born out of wedlock. Furthermore, my mind was consumed with dread that under the pressures of parenthood Little John would revert back to his dangerous habits. But at the moment of receiving the news, John and I did not respond as if the news of a baby was bad. As a pro-life advocate, I could never feel that way about a birth announcement. Instead, we talked about God's sovereign will, personal responsibility, and called upon our son for a plan of action to do the right thing. I felt an unexpected excitement about being a grandparent. So I pushed aside all my fears and doubts and relied on God.

Our precious granddaughter, Alivia Katherine Maher, was born August 5, 2005. A month later, our entire family gathered together for the special event of my husband's retirement party. However, in the weeks leading up to that evening I noticed that Little John seemed unnaturally anxious. I attributed it to his new responsibilities as a dad. Additionally, the return of his brothers could sometimes inspire apprehension in John because their successes made him question his own self-worth.

I listened to him pace the floor, night after night. I observed as he became increasingly jumpy. I began to investigate. I interrogated his cousins, who were close in age, if they had heard that John was using again. The feedback hit me like a bomb. I talked to John about it immediately, especially in light of the fact that he was now a daddy. He assured me it wasn't a problem; that he was sorry; that he had slipped temporarily; but not to worry; he was fine. Oddly, on the surface, I believed him.

It was easy to rationalize because John had done well for two years. Yet, unease, suspicion, and watchful vigilance reappeared in my demeanor like the blooming of hives following an allergic exposure. I tracked his spare time and monitored his every movement. All of the old agonizing tension fell right back into line as if it had never left.

> VOICE OF TRUTH: WHEN YOU LOVE YOUR CHILD, IT'S HARD TO BE OBJECTIVE. FOLLOW YOUR GUT, AND DON'T ALLOW YOUR EMOTIONS TO OVER-RULE WHAT YOU OBSERVE.

December 14 was a Wednesday, and at our church's midweek services that night I led the parenting class. This class was always packed with nervous young parents, but on this night during the busy holiday season only a small group of seven showed up. Like everyone else, I was overloaded with seasonal tasks, and I had not adequately prepared for class. In the absence of a ready lesson, I had decided to wing it and invite the class to share any questions or concerns they might wish to discuss.

When I faced the few in number, the intimacy of the small group steered me in a different direction and I found myself speaking frankly about my oldest son. I shared a story with them, telling how I had stayed awake half the night waiting for my son to come home, with my prone body craned and my ears attuned to hear him come through the front door. At last, in utter frustration and swamped in exhaustion, I got out of bed and walked downstairs to look out the window only to find him asleep on the sofa. He had come home several hours earlier, but I had not heard him. I told this group of parents that after all the talk I do about "trusting God" with your children, I still didn't trust and had wasted a good night's sleep for no good reason.

The parents enjoyed teasing me—they joked and called me a fraud. I agreed and felt disgusted with myself, but I was determined to win the battle over fear. I told the group that I was quitting all the worry and truly giving John up to God once and for all. I left class that night feeling strong and committed. I meant it!

I was about to be tested that very night.

When I got home, it was apparent that something wasn't right when I saw John emerge from the bathroom after an inordinate amount of time. His eyes did not look right, and he avoided eye contact with me. When I asked him, "John, are you doing drugs?", he did not answer and quickly skirted around me. In the short time I took to make a phone call to his father, he was gone—out the door and away in the car, without a shirt on a freezing cold night in mid-December.

After just declaring to my parenting class that I wasn't going to travel that ceaseless route of fear and worry anymore, here I was—thrust into a frightening situation in which I was helpless. I started to pray—the alternative was to panic. I asked the Lord at that very moment with all heartfelt sincerity to help me pass this test. I pleaded, "Lord, you heard my discussion in class tonight. I don't want to fail. Please help me. Lord, I need someone to call and pray with me. I am so fearful for John. Help me, Lord."

After our exchange on the phone, my husband had already gone to look for our son. Out of the blue, my phone rang. On the other end was a dear friend of mine. Debbie had been at the parenting class and had a question about our class discussion. Amazing—the perfect person to call me and a direct answer to my prayer.

I told Debbie what was going on. I asked her to pray with me so I could be done with all the fear. I knew from the moment the phone rang the Lord was with me. When Debbie and I hung up, I felt perfect peace.

When my husband came home and reported his lack of success in finding John, I simply said, "I'm going to bed." I was determined not to waste any more energy worrying; I was determined not to fail this test. Not this time, not again!

I slept like a baby.

CHAPTER TWO

THE TIDAL WAVE HITS

did it. That was my first waking thought as my eyes
met the blinking red numbers of my alarm clock early
the next morning. I had resisted the urge to panic; I had
passed the test. No fearsome worries, no frantic pacing,
no attempts to call my son through the night, no anxious interruptions of my slumber. I had slept!

My next move was to check Little John's bedroom
in hopes that he had slipped in during the night and
was safely asleep under his own covers. But he had not
returned home. I tried to contact him by cell phone. He
was due at work, and I knew this would be a light day
for him—it was the day of the employees' Christmas
party. When I couldn't reach him, I convinced myself
that he had slept out and then gone straight to work. I
remembered that John was going to the 76ers game that
weekend with some friends from work; this reassured
me that regardless how this latest scenario played out,
he would definitely show up at home to get the tickets.

I had plenty to do that morning because I was
helping with our church's annual Christmas program to

be held that evening. My mind momentarily shifted to how much we had to look forward to with this Christmas season upon us. I felt excitement as I anticipated Anthony and Matt coming home for the holidays. Anthony, 26, would be coming from California, where he was playing professional soccer, and Matthew, 21, in his junior year at Temple University, would be home for his winter break. Michael, 23 years old, would not be home this year because he was deployed to Iraq with the Navy.

I wasn't overly worried about John (or Michael). Had I truly arrived at a new level of trusting God? I fixed my mind on the best and most exciting news in the Maher household: celebrating Alivia's first Christmas. Eagerness for this event had us prematurely place a pile of gaily wrapped presents for her under the tree. This was obviously for our delight since she was only 4 months old.

As I went about my busy morning, my mind dwelled on these good things: a new baby in the house, the boys' return home, and the sheer pleasures of the season. Life on the surface appeared to be good; but hidden from my eyes, the solid ground had convulsed and the storm surge of a tidal wave was about to hit our home like none other.

It was about 10 A.M. when I tried several times to direct-connect John on his cell phone. At one point, I thought I heard a clicking sound and light breathing. I spoke again, "John, are you there? Please pick up."

It was part of John's personality as well as characteristic of our struggle with him that if he had failed in some way, he would slip into hiding for a while—go underground. But I felt a godly confidence this day. I had passed the test and slept through the night. I had gotten on my knees and given John over to God. I reminded myself that we had been through this drill many, many times before. He probably stayed out too late, overslept at a friend's house, and would nonchalantly walk through the door at any moment with the attitude that he didn't want to hear anything about missing work—because it was just a party day after all. He would reply to my persistent questions that worrying was my problem, not his. Been there, done that. I vowed to stay the course and trust that God was in control, not me.

While I had definitely not fallen into worry mode, my thoughts still wandered: *Was it too much to expect a courtesy phone call in order to have peace of mind if he wasn't coming home?* But relying on the evidence of my restful night, I resolved that there would be no more tossing and turning, no more fretful waiting to hear the key in the lock. I had passed the test and was excited to be in that place of total dependency on God.

So, upon finishing up my notes for the evening's church event, I calmly hit the direct-connect button on the phone for one more try. "John, are you there? Please pick up."

The unfamiliar voice on the other end startled me. "Ma'am, this is the state police. Is this your son's cell phone?"

I had the sudden sensation of heat flowing through my body as my heart pumped strenuously. My mind raced to process the words "*state police.*" "Yes," I said. "Is my son OK?"

The reply was firm. "Ma'am, we're on our way to your home, and we will be there in thirty minutes."

I repeated, "Is my son OK?"

The unwavering response, "We'll be there in thirty minutes."

With shaking hands, I called my husband at work. As an officer of the law, surely he would know what portentous news this visit could bring. His secretary told me he was in a meeting. In my ears was the thumping sound of my pulse; it seemed to be getting louder as my throat went dry. I forced my mouth to form the request, "Please interrupt him and put him on the phone."

John told me he wasn't sure what the phone call meant. After many years in law enforcement, my husband knew exactly what that call meant. He just didn't have the heart to tell me.

What could have happened to him this time? I presumed that John had gotten into trouble, and the police were bringing him home as a courtesy to my husband. It made sense, given John's public struggles with depression and drug use.

I rushed upstairs to take a shower. Afterward, I called a friend, who was a prayer partner with me, because I was becoming increasingly uneasy. I relayed to her the brief exchange with the state trooper. I said, "Ingrid, something is majorly wrong. I don't know what to expect, but I have a feeling it's not good."

Suddenly, there was a knock at my front door. My niece, Gina, stood on the porch, looking bewildered. We referred to Gina as John's "twin cousin" because they were born on the same day and were very close to each other.

As soon as I opened the door, she shouted, "What's wrong?"

Equally bewildered and panicked, I said, "Why? What's wrong?" *Why is she here? What does she know? Who called her?* It was out of the ordinary for Gina to just show up at my house. She explained that my sister Denise had called her and told her to get to my house. Uncle John (my husband) had called Aunt Dee and told her to get to my house right away to be with me. But Denise was at work; while she waited for someone to relieve her, she called Gina and sent her to my home.

Why would my husband tell my sister Denise to get over here? I knew that something was not right, but with each passing minute I had a growing alarm that something was tragically wrong. At that moment, an un-marked police car pulled into my driveway. Through my front window, I could make out two figures in the front seat. Gina looked out the window and said with relief, "John's in the car." I thought I saw the same thing. A different kind of alarm immediately set in as I wondered what kind of situation we would be facing as a fam-ily. *What kind of trouble had John gotten himself into? What would become of his job? How would this impact the life of his daughter, Alivia?* My mind was awash in anxious questions.

A closer look revealed the two persons to be men dressed in suits. It was soon clear that John was not with them, and an awful sense of dread overcame my whole being. I opened the door and asked the trooper, "What's wrong? Where is my son?"

One of the troopers responded with a question I realized was a stalling tactic. "Is your husband home?"

Despite feeling agitated and tense, my voice re-mained calm as I answered, "No. My husband is not here. And I am a praying woman, so I can handle what you have to tell me."

Continuing to buy time and allow my husband to get home, the trooper asked, "Can we step into your kitchen?"

"Yes, but tell me: Where is my son?"

"We need to ask you about your four sons."

My four sons? I couldn't imagine what the trooper meant by that. Confusion reigned. My mind churned with possible scenarios, but none made any logical sense. I couldn't imagine what was going on or why he asked about our other sons.

Then the trooper threw me with another query. "What did your son have on when he left the house?"

I described John's blue jeans and white sneakers. Just then my husband walked in and shook hands with the troopers in our kitchen. I noted his pale, somber face. The troopers turned their attention to him, and the conversation resumed man-to-man in a cold, professional manner.

Once again, they asked about our other sons. John told them in a matter-of-fact tone that Anthony was in California, Michael was on deployment in the Persian Gulf, and Matthew was at Temple University. It was apparent that those details confirmed their suspicions. In a straightforward manner, the trooper stated, "The body we found had a Navy soccer sweatshirt on."

The body we found. DID HE JUST SAY "THE BODY"?

I will never forget the dialogue that followed and the weight of the words that fell heavily on my chest. Boulders pressed upon me and squeezed me on every side. Breathing became difficult, strained, and labored. "The body we found." My son was dead.

SLAMMED!

CHAPTER THREE
STAYING AFLOAT

LIFE PRESERVER: "My grace is sufficient for you, for My strength is made perfect in weakness" (II Corinthians 12:9).

Anyone who has ever been hit with a tragedy—terminal illness, financial losses, divorce, violence or even death—knows that when the unexpected strikes, one is overwhelmed with hopelessness and despair. Life comes to a halt. A glance outside the window reveals the shining sun, the chirping birds, the scampering squirrels, and the traffic on the roadway that shows life continuing for others; but it all becomes backdrop to the sadness enveloping you like a shroud. You would almost prefer that it rain every day so at least the elements would match the state of your soul. Light seems to mock the darkness in your heart, and you long to hide away, disappear or at least fade into the background. You know your life is forever altered, and fear of the future invades every thought—debilitating you until you are so crippled you cannot function.

LIFE PRESERVER: "[B]ringing every thought into captivity to the obedience of Christ" (II Corinthians 10:5).

The first three days following the news that my son was dead found me in a state of catatonic depression. When alone, I moaned, groaned, and sighed. At night, I tossed the covers on and off my body, trying to unload the subliminal weight that covered me from head to toe. I was restless, but my repetitive movements had no purpose. My heart suffered bouts of arrhythmia while my mind was fixed in a trance-like vacuum of sadness.

I didn't want to be left alone with my emotions, but I didn't want to engage in meaningless conversation either. My husband and I barely said anything to each other for days, as we were both grieving in our own separate worlds. For the first time in our married lives, I couldn't help him and he couldn't help me. Neither of us had the strength or the energy.

For me, this doubled the pain and suffering because I had always relied on my husband to fix things. And if he couldn't fix or eliminate the problem, he would definitely walk me through it. This time, he had nothing to offer. His firstborn son had died, his namesake, and there was nothing he could do to change it.

John took on the onerous tasks related to preparing a body for burial. He identified Little John's body at the morgue. He picked out John's clothes and even dressed him for the viewing. He made all the funeral arrangements—and found himself alone as he stared at a death certificate that had his own name staring back at him. He had valued his role as provider and protector; now that self-image shattered to the ground. In the end, he felt he failed his first child—he had been unable to provide something essential, unable to protect him.

And I had nothing to offer my husband. I stayed away from the funeral preparations. I remained in my home, my body frozen and unable to move while the house was swarmed with well-intentioned people whose animated conversation nevertheless turned the atmosphere into a macabre carnival. My brain had seized—I couldn't think or process words. I just followed directions and nodded when it seemed appropriate. And so, as a couple heretofore happily married for 30 years, John and I had to traverse the devastating landscape by different routes and hope that in the end we would arrive at the same place.

My body reacted to the mental blow as if I had the flu. I felt physically ill and ached all over. John experienced the same dubious pains. For weeks after the funeral, we sat numbly in our living room—each on a recliner, gazing mindlessly at the television. Occasionally we glanced at one another and offered faint smiles. It was all we had to give while we bore our individual grief and sorrow.

My thoughts were senseless and scattered. I couldn't remember the simplest things. One evening, I looked at the toothbrushes in the bathroom and couldn't recall which one was mine. Utterly indifferent, I could not even be bothered to ask John. I just picked one up and used it. A full year later, my memory suddenly cleared—a sensation like re-entering the earth's atmosphere of light, oxygen, and gravity. I looked at the toothbrush in my hand and thought, *"Ooh, that's not my toothbrush."*

During the time of grief-induced memory loss, I reached for my ever-present water bottle and took a sip—instantly gagging on pine cleaner. I had picked up the wrong bottle. My blinkered mind had not been alerted by the senses—the appearance of the bottle, the color and odor of the liquid. Only the physical reflex of spitting up, rather than swallowing, the toxic chemical had prevented me from quenching my thirst with poison. I felt so foolish. Was I losing my mind?

That week, I received a phone call from a former high-school friend, whom I hadn't seen in years. She had heard about our loss; her tone was warm and empathetic. She thoughtfully kept the call short, saying she wanted to relay a simple fact to me from her husband who is a doctor. Her words greatly soothed my troubled spirit. She said, "You must know, Anne, that any major trauma, especially losing a child, is equivalent to your body being in a major car wreck." She will never know how much that piece of information meant to me. It explained the body aches, the fatigue, and the mental lapses.

> **VOICE OF TRUTH: AN EMOTIONAL TRAUMA WILL CAUSE YOUR BODY TO RESPOND AS IF IT HAD BEEN IN A MAJOR CAR WRECK.**

The mind is an amazing instrument, and the problem is that it is difficult to shut it down. Death is a horrendous shock to anyone, and I think the timing of Little John's death in December—just 10 days before Christmas—added another layer to my mental confusion. *'Tis the season to be jolly. Peace on earth, good will to men.* Death doesn't knock on your door like the Three Wise Men, bearing gifts.

Our house is one of those on the street that resembles a "Winter Wonderland" at Christmastime. The collision of two opposing spheres was profound: The festive season to celebrate the birth of God's Son, in direct contrast with the announcement of the death of our son. In a moment's time, the brightly decorated ornaments were displaced by an invisible veil of desolation. I saw the banality of the trinkets and baubles for the first time. The sparkle of the holiday season had been snuffed out, and I felt smothered, too. I don't even know who conscientiously plugged in our Christmas lights that year, but someone did because the contrast was so monumental—the lights only reminded me of the darkness that covered my heart and my home.

I continually cried out to God and pleaded with Him to help me. I kept repeating over and over in my head, *"God, help me."* For a time, those were the only words my brain could easily recognize.

> **LIFE PRESERVER:** "Cast all your care upon Him, for He cares for you" (1 Peter 5:7).

I have been a Christian for a long time. I had a disciplined lifestyle characterized by prayer, fasting, and fellowshipping with other Christians. My relationship with God had grown strong through the years of struggle that I had with John. It was in those darkest moments after my son's death that my love for God and knowledge of His Word would sustain me. Since I had spent the past years leading Bible studies and quoting Scriptures on every aspect of life, those lessons became my default setting. Though my mind was faulty and behaving badly, the biblical verses were deeply embedded and firmly fixed. I knew the moment the terrible news was delivered that the only One Who could understand me, hold me, and heal me was God. Not my husband. Not my family. Not my friends. Only God! And still, all I could muster were the words, "Help me, God."

> VOICE OF TRUTH: IT IS VITAL YOU UNDERSTAND
> THAT THE ONLY WAY I WAS ABLE TO PRESS
> FORWARD IN MY GRIEF WAS TO UTTERLY AND
> COMPLETELY LEAN ON GOD—AND AT THIS POINT
> IT WAS IN THOSE FEW SIMPLE WORDS, "HELP ME,
> GOD." THOSE WORDS WERE ALL I HAD INITIALLY.
> SO IF YOU HAVE EVEN FEWER WORDS THAN THAT
> IN THE MIDST OF YOUR CRISIS, BE ASSURED THAT
> NO MATTER WHAT YOUR RELATIONSHIP IS WITH
> GOD, HE DOES HEAR THE LONGINGS OF YOUR
> HEART.

In spite of the dark perplexity, I kept going back to my foundation. Drawn to Him, I knew with total certainty that God loved me and that He loved my son. No circumstances could touch me or Little John that did not first go through His hands. No matter what this looked like or felt like, I had to rely on the certainty that God would hold me up.

> LIFE PRESERVER: "We know that all things work together for good to those who love God, to those who are called according to His purpose" (Romans 8:28).

How could these tragic circumstances ever work together toward something "good"? I didn't understand what "purpose" this loss could serve. But my relationship with a living God dictated that I needed to embrace an eternal mindset and trust that things look much different from Heaven than they do from here. I had to rest in a faithful and trustworthy God.

> VOICE OF TRUTH: YOU MUST SEEK GOD AND ASK HIM TO REVEAL HIMSELF TO YOU. HE IS REAL. HE IS THE ALMIGHTY—THE OMNIPOTENT, THE OMNISCIENT, THE OMNIPRESENT. HE IS YOUR CREATOR, AND HE LOVES YOU—EVEN IF YOU DON'T FEEL LOVED. I WANT TO REMIND YOU OF THAT FACT. THIS IS NOT ABOUT RELYING ON YOUR EMOTIONS, BUT STANDING ON HIS PROMISES AND ALLOWING HIM TO HOLD YOU UP. FEELINGS FOLLOW FAITH.

As the days passed, I found myself talking more and more to Jesus—and my heart-to-heart wasn't all nice either. There were times I questioned and wondered how after all these years of being faithful and diligently praying for my children, how God could allow this to happen. This was not the future I had prayed for my son. I thought John was going to be a pastor. In my heart, I had waited patiently for the time I would see the fruit of his upbringing combine with victory over his struggles. I visualized him sharing his experiences and lessons learned with others facing similar situations. That vision had sustained me through all the torment of John's addiction. That is what I thought God's faithfulness looked like—a storybook happy ending. How could I have been so wrong?

John's precious daughter only added to the weight and the pain because she would never know her father; possibly, she would grow up without a father. I couldn't understand my God at this moment. But I was left with two choices: *Run away from Him or run to Him.*

There really was no choice for me because, like a builder who spent a lot of time preparing the foundation of his home, my relationship with God was the only secure footing upon which to stand. I had spent the last 20 years learning about God—and loving Him. This would sustain me. From the very beginning, those monosyllabic meditations were enough to sustain me in the moment. "I am loved." "God, you love me." "God, help me."

> VOICE OF TRUTH: IF YOU ARE IN DARKNESS AND DESPAIR, THEN YOU NEED TO TURN TO THE ONE WHO HAS OVERCOME DARKNESS AND DESPAIR. LEAN ON HIM. CHRIST WILL SHOW UP AND WALK BESIDE YOU. HE WILL QUIET YOUR MIND. HE WILL PUT HIS HAND IN YOURS AS A PARENT DOES WITH A LOST AND LONELY CHILD. HE KNOWS THE WAY OUT OF THE WOODS FOR YOU, AND HE NEEDS YOU TO TRUST HIM.

The more I quieted my being and contemplated God, the more He showed up. There were many people who became the hands and feet of God. They brought me comfort through their words, their actions, and their provisions. I was also getting much needed reassurance that my son John was in perfect peace in Heaven. I found his journal and other writings—poems and letters—that affirmed his deep love for Jesus despite his ongoing struggles. God was indeed holding me, and it was personal.

That does not mean, however, that I escaped feeling out-of-sorts for a long while. I existed in a fog—able to hear and see and even smile and converse, but the synergy was muted. I was on the outside, watching—aware even of my social self as a separate person from the truer, inner me. This is a normal response in the grieving process. Our bodies are designed to protect us from severe emotional or physical distress by putting up a shield.

But time marches on, and I had to go back to work just four weeks later. I had the obligations to supply my newspaper column and to get back into the schools, putting on the abstinence assembly programs and running after-school clubs. John, in addition to being the county undersheriff, is the head soccer coach at our local high school. Going back to work and having to "act normal"—putting on a happy face, interacting with teen-agers, and challenging those students with a message that included words like "responsibility" and "restraint"—was daunting. Especially since my son died of drug-induced hypothermia, which meant he froze to death in his car under the influence of drugs. Little John's car had run out of gas. He rolled to a stop on the shoulder of the road. At some point, he pulled on a sweatshirt he found in his car. Then he simply closed his eyes and never woke up. He didn't have any identification with him, and that is why the state troopers had inquired about all our sons—they needed to be sure "the body" was John.

To make matters worse, there is an added stigma for those of us whose loved ones have died as a result of drugs, alcohol, suicide or other consequence of unhealthy choices. The public scrutiny and judgment add strain and guilt to an already traumatic loss. We know there will be no accolades for such an ignominious death—no legacy of praise or honor because of the wonderful life the deceased had lived. Instead, the passing of this person will be acknowledged as an act of failure, a self-inflicted collapse unworthy of any attention aside from the fodder it provides for the gossip mill. If truth be told, I would have stayed inside, crawled under my bed, and not returned to the living.

> **VOICE OF TRUTH: GET UP WHEN YOU DON'T FEEL LIKE IT. *PRESS ON!***

Here is an important principle: I had to *force* myself to get out of bed every day. I began each morning quoting the following Scripture: *"This is the day the Lord has made; I will rejoice and be glad in it"* (Psalm 118:24). It was a necessary and deliberate exercise in order to get me out of bed and on with the day.

Quoting Scripture didn't make the day miraculously easy. Tears fell down my face during the entire car ride to work, and they would resume as I drove back home again. But while I was there, I put on the happy face and greeted the solemn faces that looked back at me as if nothing had happened. I wore a cheerful demeanor as if it were my protective coat of armor. To the outside world, I must have looked fine. In reality, I knew if I did not guard my emotions in these public places, one little scrape would result in a hemorrhage.

I had to find a *new normal.*

CHAPTER FOUR

A NEW NORMAL

LIFE PRESERVER: "God whispers to us in our pleasures, speaks to us in our conscience, but shouts in our pains: It is His megaphone to rouse a deaf world."—C.S. Lewis

After a trauma of any sort, a person tends to classify his or her life in sections of "pre" and "post." Everything will revert back to those markers. When trying to recall the specific timeline of an event, I instantly relate it in this way: "*Oh, that was before John died*" or "*That was after John died.*" "Remember when" crept into my conversations way too often, revealing my longing for life before the trauma.

LIFE PRESERVER: Lean into it.

The reality is: One *is* forever changed, and everything done from now on will require adaptation to a new kind of normal. It will take deliberate effort to forge this new trail. One of the most powerful chapters of a book I read on grief was titled, "Lean into the Pain."[1] Contrary to all I had assumed to be true, the grieving process was not something I could fix with a manual or a seminar. Give me a to-do list, a formula or schedule, and I will be happy to comply. Structure is my safety net, but, regrettably, this process was far from structured and definitely not safe. I imagined grief would be something to get over, to conquer. Hurry up and get it done so life can move back to normal.

I was relieved when I heard for the first time that it wasn't in my best interest to "overcome" or "solve" this situation—but simply lean into it. This concept suggested an alternate route. The exercise involved a middle ground. It wasn't suggesting I avoid grief altogether nor that I engage in the polar opposite by embracing the sadness to such a degree that I grew comfortable remaining there. Rather, this approach recommended leaning gently into the circumstance.

Life had irrevocably changed. My life had changed, and I did not believe I could ever be content or happy again for the rest of my life. My child was gone. The kitchen cupboards were lined with his favorite foods. The recliner that he commandeered the moment he walked in from work was empty. His bedroom was vacant; his shoes and clothing lay abandoned. Never again would he call. There would be no wedding. Plans made for the future were over. The massive heaviness was crushing, but there was little I could do about it. In fact, there was nothing I could do about it because nothing could bring John back.

[1.] Sharon W. Betters, Treasures in Darkness: A Grieving Mother Shares Her Heart (New Jersey: P&R Publishing, 2005), 86-107

As the fog gradually lifted, a new reality defined my existence. Daily, I ricocheted between conflicted emotions. Bursts of happiness that came from my other children and my beautiful new granddaughter were cut short by guilt that I was moving forward and life was continuing without my son. I was tempted to remain in the protective numbness afforded me in the aftermath of trauma, but another part of me wanted to fast-forward through the grief. Bizarrely, I wondered if John was hovering above—observing me and evaluating whether I really, truly cared that he was gone.

I longed for Heaven in a way that was scary at times. I would find myself driving and staring at the clouds, with the desire to drive right into them. There would be my son; there would be peace; there would be hope; and there would be an end to grief and guilt.

But it was clearly evident that I had to go on—just in a different way. I was being transformed from the core of my being, and I fought this new reality with every ounce of strength I could muster. This was not what I signed up for; I didn't choose this; I would never choose this. My family chain was broken; my heart was broken too. I was now a mom whose oldest son is deceased. This reality was suffocating, all-consuming, and the pain associated with it was often too much to bear.

> VOICE OF TRUTH: YOU WILL NOT ALWAYS FEEL THIS WAY. REMEMBER HIS LOVE FOR YOU. HE CAN BE TRUSTED WITH YOUR FUTURE. HE WALKS NEXT TO YOU. HIS PROMISES ARE TRUE. YOU HAVE BEEN GIVEN THE GIFT OF PAIN, AND ONE DAY YOU WILL COMFORT OTHERS WITH THE COMFORT YOU HAVE RECEIVED.

During the times when the grief seemed too much to bear, I called out to my Father in Heaven. I was frank; I told Him everything. I talked through my anger, fear, disappointment, and sadness. He was big enough to bear the burden. When Lazarus died, Jesus wept alongside His friends and Lazarus' sisters, Mary and Martha (John 11). Jesus already knew He would momentarily raise Lazarus from the dead, yet His heart was heavy because their hearts were heavy. Neither was God far removed from my painful journey. He was with me; He wept with me.

When I could not summon the strength to encourage myself, I sat with a cup of tea and read the Scriptures over and over again. The Word of God is the truth that sets one free because people will fail us, and that will disappoint us. Our hope must remain in God our Savior. He meets every need. He knows what we need before we even ask. He is a man acquainted with many sorrows. He comforts those who mourn. He is near to the broken-hearted. He can be trusted. My emotions could not be trusted as they varied regularly and were all over the map. I had to rely on the truth, and repeat the truth often.

So how does one lean? By making adjustments without being locked into assumptions of what things "should" look like or feel like. For instance, Anthony got married nine months after John's death, and I was adamant that there would be no traditional family portrait with the new bride and her husband surrounded by our immediate family. I could not bear the thought of that haunting reminder that one son-and-brother was missing. Instead, I included my two single sons' girlfriends in all the family shots. This less formal arrangement worked for me in my season of grief.

> VOICE OF TRUTH: DO NOT FEEL GUILTY WHEN YOU MAKE THESE JUDGMENT CALLS OR MODIFY TRADITIONS TO ACCOMMODATE YOUR NEW NORMAL. THERE IS NO "RIGHT WAY" TO NAVIGATE YOUR PRIVATE JOURNEY. YOUR PRIMARY RESPONSIBILITY IS TO REMAIN CLOSE TO YOUR FATHER IN HEAVEN AND TO MOVE FORWARD. HOWEVER SMALL THE PROGRESS MAY SEEM, IT'S STILL PROGRESS.

I realized that each time I stepped out into the real world, despite the apprehension and dread, it was progress. There was not going to come a day when I would wake up and feel ready to start working through the grief—I was working through the grief in the here and now.

Thankfully, God required nothing of me. I only had to rely on Him. In His loving mercy, He walked with me. When I rose, He was there—whether I rose with the sun or paced the floors with the moon. I trusted Him, called on Him, and allowed Him to hold me—rather than squirming in impatience or anxiety. I found His promises to be true: His mercies *are* new each morning (Lamentations 3: 22, 23); His love *never* fails (1 Corinthians 13:8).

I was reminded that the God of the universe—the all-powerful, all-knowing God was handling my ordeal. And it was not dependent on my performance—it really did not matter how many books I read to assist me in this journey or how many steps I fulfilled toward wholeness. God wasn't circulating overhead somewhere in the cosmos with a clipboard and a red pen, tallying up how many Bible studies I'd attended, how many prayers I'd uttered or how many times I'd been to church. His love and concern for me are constants. In all things, He was strengthening my heart as He refined my faults and defects. God delights in bringing about purpose from pain. It is His nature to restore and renew, and He uses adversity to bring about good in this life.

> VOICE OF TRUTH: "I'm overwhelmed." "I'm annoyed." "I'm lost." "I'm angry." "I'm not sure." "I'm damaged." "I doubt." "I've lost the ability to trust." "I'm afraid." PRAYER SUGGESTION: *Father, my heart is heavy. My mind is racing. My body feels weak, and I wish to close my eyes and never wake up. The duties expected of me seem too much, and I feel ill-equipped to walk this road set before me. I am a mess; my emotions are out of control. Please continue to remind me of the stability that can be found in You. You are strong enough to handle my unpredictable feelings and actions. Help me to take You at Your Word, no matter how I feel. Help me, Lord!*
>
> YOUR LIFE IS NOT OVER, BUT IT IS FOREVER CHANGED.

There was no denying that I was now and would forevermore be living with a loss, a hole in my heart, and a longing for the time before the pain, but my life was not over. It was important to me from the onset that I rely on the fact that God was in complete control of my life, regardless of the circumstances or the outcomes. This event was now part of the person I would become. It does not define me; it does not overshadow all that previously defined me. I am now a person who has experienced the death of my oldest child. It is part of my story. I am not happy about it; but "it is what it is," and I must maintain perspective.

However, there was no denying that I had changed. I realized just how much I had changed when routine conversations that used to be stimulating and engaging instead annoyed and frustrated me with the mind-numbing mundane: tedious ramblings about vacation plans; delicious meals and/or poor service at a restaurant; the wins and losses of sport teams. Sitting through the discussion of such tiresome topics would have me silently screaming, *Get over it! Get a real problem.*

I nodded when necessary. I chuckled good-naturedly when appropriate. But I was far from an active participant in these conversations. I knew that my frustration and querulous attitude were my problem, not my companions'. I could not realistically expect the rest of the world to pause while I groped my way through this unanticipated journey. Unfortunately, my logical, reasonable side did not always trump my erratic, emotional side; but most of the time I had enough clarity to remind myself to look at the big picture and to focus on my Father in Heaven, not on people.

People often won't "get it," and I came to expect them to do one or more of the following:

1. Say insensitive comments.
2. Appear heartlessly unaware of the depth of the pain.
3. Underestimate the strength required to function on the most basic level.
4. Neglect to anticipate or meet my needs.
5. Avoid me entirely.
6. Pretend nothing has happened.

That is all perfectly normal because *their* lives are still normal—they are still functioning in the "pre" or "before" era, and *I* am the one who was forcibly removed from that stage. I resigned myself to acceptance, albeit weary acceptance. I appreciated those who did "get it" and shrugged my shoulders about those who missed the mark through no fault of their own. I understood better than most that life is just too short to dwell on the misguided actions of others.

Another harrowing trap for people who have been slammed is to "check out" of life altogether, emotionally speaking—becoming distant and detached. My remaining family, however, made me unwilling to consider that option—particularly my beautiful granddaughter whose father was now dead. For the sake of these beloved ones, I had to survive. And for the sake of my deceased loved one, too, as I knew Little John would not want me to stop living.

Self-pity can be a pit of temptation into which many fall. I would feel myself slipping at times, especially when I thought of Alivia, whose own story would include the tale of her father's death. No child should have to grow up that way, bearing that pitiable distinction. But I also recognized that self-pity is the desire to make the world bear one's burden, and I steered clear of getting into those treacherous feelings.

> VOICE OF TRUTH: NOT EVERYONE "GETS IT."
> LOWERING YOUR EXPECTATIONS WILL MINIMIZE
> DISAPPOINTMENT. PEOPLE WILL DISAPPOINT
> YOU AND FAIL YOU. GOD WILL NEVER DISAP-
> POINT YOU OR FAIL YOU.

Hence, routine tasks and ordinary social interactions seemed disagreeable, too much to ask of me. In the beginning, I would rather have stayed home in the shelter of my isolation, and I had just enough energy to tackle the simplest tasks. For example, I avoided the grocery store, and I didn't have the interest required to cook. My youngest son, Matt, came home from college on the weekends and shopped for me. He also did some cooking. When I did resume the chore of food shopping, I couldn't bear to buy certain treats because they reminded me of John. Just looking at his favorite items on the shelves—tortilla chips and salsa, ice cream or yogurt—caused waves of sorrow to flood my heart. I walked the aisles hiding my tears, fighting for composure, avoiding eye contact at all costs so that I would be spared the encounter of a familiar face. Eventually the sting subsided, although I will always bear the scar.

> VOICE OF TRUTH: WHEN DIFFICULT EMOTIONS SURFACE, WALK THROUGH THEM. EVERY PART OF ME WANTED TO ABANDON MY CART AND RUN TO MY CAR. MY BED WAS THE SAFEST PLACE. BUT THE MORE YOU WALK THROUGH THESE UNCOMFORTABLE EVENTS, THE FARTHER YOU TRAVEL IN YOUR JOURNEY TOWARD HEALING. FORGE NEW ROADS.

I changed our family traditions and made new ones. We used to have an Open House on Christmas Eve. It was a gathering for our entire extended family, our church family, co-workers, community associates, neighbors, and all our friends—including our sons' friends. In the years after John's death, I lost the will to continue; now we join my brother's family for Christmas Eve. It was hard to understand and even harder to express, but I didn't have the same motivation—it didn't feel right. So part of the journey was forging new roads.

I was not compelled to keep old patterns, old routines, and old customs.

My husband and I found a surprising peace by going away on weekends. Leaving the area, getting away from the familiar, took some of the pressure off. It brought a healthy sense of relief and renewal. New York became a favorite visiting destination—emblematic of my evolving persona: I could engage shoulder-to-shoulder with humanity, yet remain separate and apart among the teeming masses.

> VOICE OF TRUTH: GET IN THE HABIT OF FORCING YOURSELF TO TRY THINGS DESPITE YOUR FEELINGS. IF YOU DON'T FEEL STRONG ENOUGH TO DO THIS, ASK A RELIABLE FRIEND TO HELP YOU. THE ALTERNATIVE IS TO STAY MIRED IN THE SADNESS. FIND A PURPOSE.

Because of my faith in God, I wrestled with the idea of finding a bigger purpose in this tragedy. I knew it was an opportunity to really live out my faith in the sight of my children. I mean, it is easy to say, "God does all things well" when all things are well. But in the center of a storm, how would I articulate that truth to others?

As time moved on, I prayed for the Lord to give me an opportunity to press forward—showing others what I knew in my head, but couldn't quite grasp yet in my heart: that God is real; that He loves us; that He provides peace. It had to be a deliberate exercise of my will to face my circumstances optimistically, recite all of the other provisions God had tended to in my life, and acknowledge His complete control. When I did this, my sadness over this terrible loss became manageable.

Throughout the first couple years of grieving, the Lord strengthened me in ways I never thought possible. One result was that I grew more compassionate; I became more aware and more responsive to other people's pain. The circumstances of our son's death dismantled the "all-American perfect family" illusion; in the wake of that, numerous opportunities opened up to minister to suffering parents going through similar struggles with their children.

> LIFE PRESERVER: "Blessed be the God and Father of our Lord Jesus Christ, the Father of mercies and God of all comfort, who comforts us in our tribulation, that we may be able to comfort those who are in any trouble, with the comfort with which we ourselves are comforted by God"
> (1 Corinthians 1:4).

A traumatic event has the ability of providing a better perspective of what's really important in life. For me, that meant ministering to other people who were facing pain. If I heard of someone in distress, I made a mental note of it. Later, I would take the time to write a letter, send an e-mail or text an encouraging word. In turn, I was helped as I found myself gaining strength through these acts.

VOICE OF TRUTH: REPRIORITIZE YOUR SCHEDULE.

For a long time, I grew stronger from the confines of my home, from my solitude with God. I resigned from teaching the parenting class. I couldn't face the young parents who had regularly attended through the years. I was certain they were thinking I was a fraud and a failure—and I couldn't blame them if they did. Undoubtedly, I would have felt that way when I was a young parent—when black and white were the only options, and outcomes always matched input. To have a son die under the influence of drugs had to be the result of parental malfunction or family dysfunction. That would have been my own conclusion—surely it was theirs.

I resigned from teaching Sunday school and from my seat on the church board. I didn't write a column for the newspaper for one full year. I withdrew for the purposes of rest and refreshment. This was precisely what Jesus had done. He would periodically withdraw from the crowds and go into isolation in order to draw strength from His Father. Temporary periods of withdrawal are necessary for the re-energizing process.

I read every book I could get my hands on that was intended to strengthen my spiritual muscles and encourage me forward. I immersed myself in spiritual music; listening to the lyrics that sang the yearnings of my own heart ministered to me in a new way. And I took time to be quiet and listen to the still small voice of my God.

LIFE PRESERVER: "Be still, and know that I am God" (Psalm 46:10).

It was necessary that I take this time to retreat. I thrived in the quiet place, where I could heal and begin the transition from paralysis to purpose. I still had my everyday work obligations and duties to perform. In between teaching the abstinence curriculum in the public schools, I watched Alivia at our house while her mother worked.

The circumstance of replacing Little John in Alivia's life was confusing to me, and added another element for which I needed to find a healthy balance through this whole process. I felt bound to Alivia, and her well-being absorbed all of my concentration.

VOICE OF TRUTH: THE CHANGED CIRCUMSTANCES IN YOUR LIFE CAUSED BY YOUR TRAUMA WARRANT YOU TO FIND HEALTHY CHECKS AND BALANCES. IT IS A NECESSITY TO SEEK TRUSTED FRIENDS WHO CAN BE HONEST AND TRANSPARENT WITH YOU. I BOUNCED MY CONFUSED EMOTIONS OFF MY SISTER AND A FEW CLOSE FRIENDS. IT HELPED ME SORT OUT THE NORMAL FROM THE OBSESSIVE. IT WAS MY LIFELINE IN THE MOMENT.

My daily schedule was draining. Even well-meaning friends, family, and church members added to my exhaustion with their frequent visits. They were sweetly attempting to minister to me, but I needed the peace of the solitary.

After two years of trying to find the balance between the need for stillness and the demands of my daily life, my 10-year job as an abstinence educator abruptly came to an end when the State abolished the federally funded program. On principle and for the sake of our co-workers dependent on the income, I was sorry; but for myself, I was relieved. I was now free to stay at home and take full control of my and Alivia's daily routine. I could rest in the peaceful quiet of my new schedule. This was just another way that I saw God's grace and mercy intimately answering the deep issues and concerns of my heart.

VOICE OF TRUTH: TEND TO YOUR SPOUSE.

These two years of mourning brought my husband and me closer than ever before. I believe that is because we were carefully observant toward each other's needs. He began to call me during the day to see how I was doing. If I didn't hear from him, it was a sure sign that I needed to call him and see if he was OK. We talked about our emotions. I am Type A, the gabby partner, and he is more introspective and disinclined to reveal his feelings. So, I freely shared my pain with him and asked that he do the same so there would be no walls between us. He honored my request, even if the discussion was out of character for him and occasionally discomfiting.

My close friend, April Lassor, pulled me aside just days after Little John's death and carefully shared a few words of counsel. April had lost her 12-year-old son, Matthew, in a tragic car accident. She told me that in spite of the pain, do not forget that our husbands relate to us on a different level; they place a high priority on sex. The priority that a woman places on emotional oneness is the priority that a man places on physical oneness; thus, a woman's emotional needs are matched by her husband's physical needs. While it's probable that a woman in mourning would be distracted from thinking about sex, it is her man's way of drawing comfort.

I listened to what April had to say, even if it did somewhat startle me, and I learned that she was right. In spite of my emotions being oriented in another way, I knew I had to keep the lines of communication open between John and me—which, for a man, entails much more than words.

So we both prioritized the other and paid attention to each other's needs. There is nothing more special than making it through as a team. Our common grief and shared loss had bound us in ever more deeper ways. And the sadness was recasting us both in the same mold, moving us in the same direction of greater sympathy for others in pain.

LIFE PRESERVER: "Two are better than one [...] for if they fall, one will lift up his companion" (Ecclesiastes 4:9-12).

There is something very fulfilling about being transparent after you've been slammed. After a full year of isolation from the community, I felt ready to write my first column. I could not resume my hiatus from writing as if nothing had happened in my life. If I was going to return to a place of public exposition, I had to continue to be the relational person the readers had come to expect. I had to write what was on my heart, even if it meant exposing some tender wounds.

The following is my column, published December 6, 2006.

Recently, I have run into several people who have kindly told me how much they enjoy reading "Family Matters" each month. I am flattered, but don't want to embarrass them by admitting I haven't written the column in about a year. Perhaps for them – as it is for me – time just passes so quickly that one month blends into another.

This past year of seasonal changes and cyclical moon phases nevertheless merged into the biggest blur yet of my 50 compiled years. Since receiving the shock of my life, the news that my oldest son had suddenly passed away, I have been struggling to make sense of my skewered vision. As if, on Dec. 15, 2005, a haze fell over my eyes, and all that I had taken for granted about my surroundings suddenly became a foggy, fuzzy, incomprehensible landscape.

Functioning on autopilot all this time, I am only now landing on the reality that a full year has passed; and I am perplexed by the heart-wrenching question of how this could be.

The death of a loved one, particularly your child, changes everything. It is an illogical, incongruent notion for a parent to bury a child – out of step with the natural order for life.

The whole family dynamic is changed. A void is created, which redefines everyday life and produces a dread of future momentous occasions without that person present. You view the world differently through tear-stained eyes.

I have had to learn to cope with the huge, hollow, aching space in the pit of my stomach. It can never be filled for the rest of my time here on earth. I face each new day with an abiding sadness of missing my son. I long to hear his voice, catch a glimpse of his smile or share some meaningful moment with him.

Intensifying my anguish in the most immediate days after his death was the painful reality that his 4-month-old daughter would never know her father. But as I was privileged to assist in the baby-sitting responsibilities for my granddaughter, a paradoxical miracle took place within my heart: where a shoot of joy was planted alongside the shoot of grief. These two opposing emotions were cultivated in me, and somewhere in the process their branches have become intertwined and will forever be a part of one another.

It was at those times when fear of the future would begin to choke me that I would get to stare at her beautiful, serene face; my heart would overflow with the familiarity of her expression, for she looks just like her dad. Like any proud grandmother, I am fixated by her tiny little mannerisms – her tongue dangling from her mouth when she is busy at play, but it seems more wondrous and captivating since that gesture was her daddy's trademark when he was a toddler. I revel in the shape of her fingers – hands I recognize and held many years ago.

I continually thank God for giving our family such a gift in the midst of such a storm. She is a living part of our son that only increases our joy as she matures and serves in a vital way in keeping his future alive.

The initial phases of grief are like a tidal wave drowning your every thought and leaving you feeling paralyzed, helpless, and without control. But unlike those who grieve without hope, I have seen my Lord's faithful hand orchestrated in every minute detail of this story.

I have learned more this year about God's faithfulness than at any other time in my life. He has chosen to take me into a deep, dark valley; and in it I have met him more personally and intimately. I have been comforted by the people he sends my way on a daily basis. I know there will continue to be many hard and difficult times – the impending holidays, for instance – but I will face them with my heart and mind focused on eternal matters ... for after all, it is in that eternal place that I will meet my son once again.

That column was the beginning of my resumption of public life in a new and different way. The response to the column confirmed that there are many hurting people out there who are suffering with their pain. Their feedback encouraged me to continue writing, continue living, continue making a difference. I knew I could do it, I wanted to do it, and I felt the Lord was guiding me to do it. I was getting better.

> **VOICE OF TRUTH: YOU WON'T ALWAYS FEEL THIS WAY.**

Time does have a way of making the wound more bearable. I remember the first Christmas, just two weeks after John died, April was at my house. She looked at me across the room, and with that single glance she understood my expression of utter desolation. She walked over and whispered in my ear, "It won't always feel this way." At that moment, knowing the pain of her own loss yet seeing her strength in her characteristic serenity, I believed her. Her words breathed life into me.

Time makes the wound more bearable because, like a bloody injury, it eventually scabs over and takes on a different form. The scar will always be there as a reminder of the infliction. Time serves its purpose by widening the crevasse between the insatiable yearning for what has been lost and the reality of a changed world so that the memory can take on distance and perspective. Pain, however, is always part of loss.

I was into my third year of the grief journey when I began to feel better—as recovered, I felt, as it was possible to be. It was December, 2008, when I got a call from a former co-worker regarding funds for a new abstinence program. She wanted to know if I would like to teach it. I was excited. *I am ready to get back into the swing of things.* I felt that God had transformed me through these last three years, and now I wanted to return to the work about which I was passionate. Alivia was now in preschool three days a week, and I was free to arrange my teaching schedule on those days. I accepted, and the new position began in February.

It was invigorating. Those three years had had me on the back side of a desert, and now I was emerging with a newfound appreciation for life. I enjoyed teaching and interacting with the high-school students, and it was gratifying to use John's story in the drug-and-alcohol segments of the curriculum. His death had the strange advantage of giving me and the abstinence message more credibility with the students. I was thankful to God for enabling me to be transparent and use the story, even if it hurt. I felt a greater purpose was at work as I prepared the curriculum and program logistics.

The excitement of the holiday season was once again upon us. Christmas will always be a dreadful reminder, but that year Alivia was 3 and gleefully anticipating the arrival of Santa. Her enthusiasm definitely infused our home with a fresh spark.

Then, on December 11, 2008, I received a disturbing phone call that my mother had had a minor heart attack in Florida, where she and my father were tying up loose ends in preparation for moving permanently into their attached suite in my house. My dad's ailing health had precipitated the decision to sell their Florida residence. Here, in New Jersey, they would be steps away from us, on the other side of our enclosed breezeway, and nearer to the rest of my siblings as well.

Mom was a busy, active, and high-spirited 74-year-old, who religiously walked five or more miles a day. She was in excellent shape; her body was strong and robust. While the news was troublesome, I wasn't overly worried. I was confident when I went to bed that Mom's grit and tough Italian genes would pull her through, and I would speak to her in the morning. I said a prayer for her as my head hit the pillow, and then I slept soundly.

I would never hear her voice again. During a routine procedure, a blood clot had caused complications, which led to a deprivation of oxygen to her brain. She was brain-dead, while her otherwise healthy organs hung on for several arduous weeks.

SLAMMED!

Once again, throughout the Christmas season, I felt the weight of sadness and loss. For Christians, the season officially ends January 6, called Epiphany or Three Kings' Day. In some cultures, the day is called "Little Christmas" and includes another round of gift-giving. For me, in 2009, the day held another surprise.

In the early hours of January 6, the telephone rang with the news—Mom had passed. I cried with relief that she was finally free of the agony of the last few weeks. Her horrendous ordeal had been surreal and grotesque.

Once again, the experience of sudden and unexpected death, the replacement of celebratory reunion with saying good-bye at a funeral, tore off my scabs and reopened the wound. Nightmares and sleepless nights revisited me, and the sadness of my heart was visible on my face. I walked through my parents' apartment—once filled with the tantalizing aromas of Mom's famous Italian cooking—and wept at the sight of the new bedspread she had bought and never used. She didn't want to sleep with it until she came back, she had said, so everything would feel new. On the day they left for Florida, I remembered how Mom had made up the bed and neatly placed the bedspread on top, and then stood with hands on hips to survey the perfectly appointed apartment that would welcome them when they returned. I felt silly—sobbing at the sight of a bedspread that my mother had excitedly kept in store for the future; and then that future wobbled and fell. I was struck again by the knowledge that life is short—even for a woman in her 70s. My heart was heavy for my father, too, as I watched him try to go on without his wife, who had been by his side for the past 54 years.

Two months later, March 7, 2009, another catastrophic tsunami would hit our family. This time, the colossal tidal wave came without any of the signs and early warnings that had marked John's life before he died, and was far more unpredictable than the passing of an aged woman.

That morning, our house was rocked by another unthinkable phone call. On the other end was my husband's superior, Sheriff Gary Shaffer. His news would knock me down, sweep me under, and flip my world upside down all over again.

SLAMMED!

CHAPTER FIVE
HELP, I'M DROWNING

Any lifeguard will attest that the most dangerous victim to assist in the water is the one who is trying to save himself. Struggling swimmers scrambling to stay afloat will hamper the rescue effort and potentially cause others to drown by grabbing onto them and pulling them under. The best way to survive is to totally surrender to the care of the person providing aid. It is not easy to do because it is a natural instinct to fight for breath; the instinct for self-preservation assures that we fight to survive.

When this particular wave hit, I plummeted to the depths of the ocean floor. There was not a flotation device in sight, and had there been one, I wouldn't have grabbed hold of it. I wanted to just keep sinking deeper and deeper until all signs of life were vanquished. I was about to lose my youngest son—not to physical death, but death to all he was until this one fateful night.

Matthew was 24 years old. As the youngest, he enjoyed the special and unique position of the baby of the family—treasured, adored, and excused. He graduated from Temple University Fox Business School with a concentration in Legal Studies. His brothers excelled in sports and academics, and Matthew was no different. It was apparent at a young age that he had the best traits of all the boys—as if their finest attributes had been culled and instilled in his genes. Taking up the rear in birth order, he had the advantage of training with not one coach, but four—Dad plus three brothers.

In high school, his brothers' reputations afforded Matt instant acceptance, but as a remarkable athlete he soon stood out on his own. By his junior year, he was captain of both the soccer and basketball teams. He broke school records on the soccer field and led the basketball team to back-to-back titles, including a state championship. He was "that guy"—the one that stepped to the line to sink the much-needed foul shot in a high-pressure basketball game, and the one to be put in the position of taking the critical penalty kicks in a soccer match.

Matt was president of his public high-school's Bible Club. His exuberance and confidence placed him well above any concerns about peer pressure. Without embarrassment, Matt accompanied me to schools throughout our area, where he spoke eloquently about his decision to remain abstinent. Younger students looked up to him as a role model. He was featured in commercials that were aired during local sporting events, in which he encouraged other teen-age guys to be "real men" and resist the pressure to have sex. Matt stood up for what he believed in, and he had the respect of his peers.

In college, Matt was the captain of his soccer team. As a freshman, he made the Atlantic 10 Conference All-Rookie Team. In his senior year, he was selected as a Philadelphia Soccer Seven All-Star. That same year, he was drafted to play professional soccer in the first round by Miami FC. He declined that offer in order to finish his education. Upon graduation, he was drafted in the first round by the N.J. Ironmen of the Major Indoor Soccer League (MISL), a position he accepted. That summer, he played outdoor soccer with the Carolina Railhawks (USL), earning a reputation as an up-and-coming pro to watch. Eventually he was traded to the Philadelphia Kixx, where he joined his brother and fellow pro soccer player Anthony as a teammate.

Matt always made us proud. He was the dynamic center that drew in our entire extended family, open with his affections toward one and all. His infectious humor, ticklish sense of fun and delight, and good nature made us all laugh and united us through the joys and the sorrows. He never went through any awkward or self-conscious phases typical of puberty—he neither rejected nor rebelled against us. He never acted ashamed to be seen in public with his parents, and he never gave us a moment's worry. To the contrary, we called him "Grandpop" because of his predictable behavior and well-organized routines.

Matt and I were very close, and others frequently commented on our unusual relationship. When I couldn't do it, he shopped and cooked for me. And he took the responsibility one step further—teaching me how to eat better, more nutritional foods. Matt had that way of making all of us—from his grandparents to the littlest babies in the family—know that we were loved and cared for.

So that phone call, and the subsequent events that unraveled our lives, hit me like another thunderous wave. This time, I did think I would never return to the surface again. It was the first time I thought: *God must surely hate me.*

March 7, 2009, was a typical Saturday morning, which meant I was busy cleaning when the phone rang at 9. Through the years of parenting four boys, and especially after the experiences of phone calls that conveyed messages of death, I instinctively keyed in on this early-morning, weekend conversation between my husband and the sheriff. Alerted by the serious tone of John's voice, I walked into the study—hoping to be assured by his body language.

John's blanched face, stiffened jaw, and deliberate avoidance of eye contact with me immediately caused my blood pressure to climb. John's career in law enforcement, with its inherent stress of urgent calls at all hours, had fostered a private code between us—signals that let me know whether I needed to be concerned. If the call was strictly work-related, he would give me a simple thumbs-up. That gesture would have said the call was not a family emergency, that it had nothing to do with the boys.

I maneuvered about the room in order to gain eye contact, but John refused to look at me. This was not the right cue that would allow me to go back to cleaning my house. With my heart beating in a frightening way, I understood there was a family-related problem at hand.

John's immediate reaction following the phone call was to bring his fist crashing down on his desk. He then turned to me and said, "Matt was driving drunk and was in an accident." Agitated, he brushed past me and went outside to make another call.

I was shocked by Matt's behaving so irresponsibly. My mind raced to recall the ramifications of a DUI (driving under the influence) charge. I was angry as I considered the shame this news would bring on his reputation. *Would he lose his license? Would his insurance be affected?*

Matt was scheduled for surgery in Philly a few days later for a torn ACL (anterior cruciate ligament) and meniscus. He had incurred these injuries the week before in a game against Rockford. His mind had been haunted by this blow to his knee, a possible career-ender. But the concerns about his future as an athlete faded in my mind while disgust and fear rose. Our family name and his father's reputation were, once again, out there in a bad way. I saw Matt's Christian testimony flushed down the toilet.

However, it seemed there was more to this accident, though I couldn't put my finger on what that might be. I followed John outside, where I watched him make a series of phone calls. Every time I tried to get close to him to listen in on the conversation, he veered in the other direction.

When John finally got off the phone, I hesitantly asked, "Where did the accident happen?"

"The Atlantic City Expressway." He tossed out that reply while moving rapidly about the house, preparing to leave.

"What is next?" I asked, and he said he was going to go pick up Matt at the state police barracks.

Married to this man for 33 years, I knew deep down that something more was going on. John has nerves of steel, but this news had thoroughly rattled him. He was preoccupied, edgy, the tension of his body humming in his rigidly taut muscles. I couldn't bring myself to question him further. I decided I would wait until we had Matt back home, and then the three of us would discuss the problem.

As I headed back inside, I saw my brother Jack pull into the driveway. Jack is a retired police detective, and our families are very tight. I watched as he and John huddled in deep conversation, then the two of them drove away together. I was glad Jack was going with John for moral support.

Before the men had even exited the driveway, I was on the phone—calling Denise and April and beseeching them to pray. I had such an uneasy feeling after hanging up the phone that I burst into tears and asked the Lord to give me strength. At this moment, I still could not reckon Matthew as a drunk driver, now under arrest.

A few hours passed. I paced frantically from room to room, waiting for the phone call from John that would update me on the details. Silence filled the air like thick ooze, and as the hours ticked by I recognized the silence as sinister. I was too afraid to dial John's cell. I knew I was waiting for bad news, so I retreated behind the wall I had erected since the death of Little John. The wall was characterized by avoidance of stress with mental tricks and diversionary tactics until I had been prepared to deal with the situation. Never again did I want to get hit with such pain—pain that went in deep and penetrated every recess of mind and body, moving in like a living, breathing entity. Hence, I was on guard.

Finally, I decided to call Anthony. I needed to know the truth. Anthony is the son who can always find the proverbial silver lining in any cloud. He is always positive, optimistic, and upbeat. I wanted him to beam his sunshiney personality onto Matt's situation and help me handle it. But after several seconds of conversation, the panic swelled within me. I regretted stepping out from behind the wall, and every ounce of my being wanted to run back and add a few more layers of protection.

Anthony's voice was strained, and he did not serve me his customary expressions of cheer: "This isn't the end of the world, Mom" or "It's not as bad as you think" or "Good will come out of it." His minimal responses were respectful, without offering any information or commentary. So I inquired directly, "Is Matt OK?"

"Mom, you should really talk to Dad."

I told him that Dad had left hours earlier, and there had been no contact since. "What do you know?" I demanded.

"Mom, call Dad."

"Is Matt hurt?" The unthinkable had entered my mind: Perhaps they are shielding me from the bad news that Matt is injured—or even dead. "Please tell me, Ant. You know Dad will protect me, but it is killing me to not know the whole story. What do you know?"

Anthony said, "Matt's not hurt."

"OK, so what else could it be?"

Reluctantly, Anthony responded, "Maybe someone else got hurt."

My stomach lurched. I had not considered that someone else might be involved. Thus far, no one else had been mentioned, and I had assumed Matt was driving alone. "Do you know who he was with?" I asked.

But Anthony had said as much as he intended to say. He ended the call by stating, "Dad will probably be home soon."

As I hung up the phone, I was consumed with more dreadful questions. *Maybe Matt's passenger is injured. Who could have been with him?* But I was too afraid to even call Denise again for fear that she knew something, and I no longer thought I could bear to hear it. Instead, I resumed aimlessly pacing the silent rooms, stopping occasionally to stare out the window in search of my husband's car.

Nausea rose from my churning stomach as I considered a potential DUI charge turning into a far more serious allegation. I felt weak, my muscles constricted. I did not have the strength to go through another painful ordeal. I held a desperate desire that the men would return soon and tell me what was going on as strongly as a desperate fear that they would return soon and tell me what was going on.

At 3:30, the car at long last pulled up in the driveway. My husband and my brother came into the house and asked me to sit down. I could see Matt getting out of the car, turning to collect his things. He looked tired and dejected, his shoulders slumped. I gave John and Jack my attention and knew by their faces that they were about to drop a bomb on me. Jack didn't waste any time because he wanted me to know before Matt walked in the door. He said, "Anne, the guy in the other vehicle died."

My head exploded. *There was another car involved.* I had not thought about that possibility either. The magnitude that a person had died did not escape me. "The body we found" are words imbedded like shrapnel in my heart. My son had died. I had lived with the pain of that for three years. Just eight weeks earlier my mom had inexplicably died. And now, someone else was dead. Someone innocent. Someone innocent was dead, and my son was responsible.

The sickness flooding my body was now accompanied by fury. *After all I have been through these past few years ... and just losing my mother ... and now this. My son, this son with the perfect life, has killed someone.* In freefall: down, down, down the rabbit hole, I went. The ramifications were too big to process.

Matt walked through the door, eyes cast down. He seemed shocked and devastated. As he headed toward the stairs and the comfort of his room, I uttered the words that welled from my sick and disgusted heart. I looked at him and said, "It should have been you."

One would think I might regret such a display of callousness. Mothers don't wish their children harm. Mothers don't say things like that. Especially, one would think, a mother who already has one dead child. Those words were contrary to all that a mother would feel in her heart. But at that moment I could not summon motherly instincts. I was only aware of my outrage. My body grew rigid with anger as I watched Matt slowly climb the stairs. I was staring at the person who had shattered my carefully reconstructed world, his own world, and the world of an innocent family. Another family was now suffering a loss because of my child's actions, and I was revolted by the thought of it.

Later I went up to his room and tried to comfort Matt, telling him we would get through this, but I did not believe the shallow words for one moment. I had been brought to my lowest point because no matter how hard I tried to concentrate on God and rely on my faith, I did not believe we would get through this. How could we? This was a terrible, irreversible tragedy—the type of horror from which people do not recover. For all the years of investing in my child, this was the result—the fruit of the labor. Shame, discouragement, and total disillusionment framed my soul. This time, these were the only words I had for God: *"My God, my God, why have you forsaken me?"*

For many days, we knew nothing about the victim because he didn't have a driver's license on him. Without a name and a history to identify the man, the facts blurred, became nebulous. I kept hoping someone would tell me there had been a mistake, a big mistake. Perhaps the police had their facts wrong; perhaps my child hadn't really killed someone. Perhaps the victim was also at fault; perhaps he had also been driving while intoxicated. Perhaps Matthew's injured knee was a contributing factor; perhaps his car malfunctioned. I had slipped into denial and was looking for any excuse, any way out of the serious consequences of reality.

My mind kept wandering back to the victim. *Who was he? Did he have a family? Was he young? Old?* I couldn't bear to know these details, yet I couldn't help wondering about the people with whom we were now forever linked.

Denise, Anthony, and our pastor showed up at the house that night. Denise went up to Matt's room, where he lay in the dark. She asked if he was OK. "I wish it was me that died," was all he said.

In our family room, Anthony sat dazed and stupefied on the sofa. He rested his head back against the cushions. In a voice of anguish and stunned disbelief, he murmured, "He's going to prison."

Reacting like a tigress bent on protecting her young, I demanded harshly, "What are you talking about? Prison! Why would you say that? It was an accident!"

It was then that I was introduced to the legalities of drunk-driving offenses. John and Jack jumped in and began discussing Matt's case in terms that were foreign to my ears: vehicular homicide; aggravated manslaughter; death by auto. From the depths of his own heartache, John explained to me that "there was a good possibility" Matt was facing a minimum of three years in prison. *Prison?* How could I make the transition from having a son at the top of his game to the news that he was likely going to prison for several years?

The news broke in the media that day, and every major network and newspaper broadcast the headline: "Philadelphia Kixx player arrested in fatal drunk driving accident." The phone began to ring; people began to arrive at our door; even flowers were sent from caring friends. Instantly, the resemblance to the feel of death was too much for my emotions. This time someone innocent had died, and my son was responsible. Matt's only words over the next few days were, "I wish it had been me."

The sight of my son's photograph next to a storyline that contained words like "fatal," "DUI," and "killed" was incomprehensible to me. Once again, the irony of avidly reading the paper and watching the TV news to see Matt's accomplishments reported for so many years juxtaposed against this latest report of another stunning deed.

Just the previous year, the brothers had implemented a community-wide soccer camp in honor of their brother, John. The camp, led and taught by professionals, was offered to children free-of-charge. It had an emphasis centered on Christ, and was called "Victory IV Jesus." The Roman numeral "IV" symbolized the four Maher brothers. There was even a John Maher Jr. award for the camper who supported others throughout the week with encouragement and a positive attitude.

I thought this was the beginning of restoring our family name. The camp enabled me to come to terms with my feelings of failure as a mother and the ever-present judgment from people (particularly those in law enforcement) because of the manner in which John died. (Though I had to admit that prior to having that stick of dynamite hurled into my home, I would have been just as judgmental as the rest of them.) And it thrilled my heart to see my boys involve themselves in such a positive way—using their gifts and witnessing to their faith for the benefit of kids and their families. Maybe the values I had taught them were worthwhile after all. Maybe the vision I had for my sons would come to fruition after all.

> VOICE OF TRUTH: REMEMBER THAT YOUR CHILDREN (AND EVERYONE IN YOUR LIFE) ARE LOVED BY GOD FAR MORE THAN YOU ARE EVEN CAPABLE OF LOVING THEM. REGARDLESS OF YOUR CIRCUMSTANCES, YOU CAN REST ASSURED THAT GOD IS NOT SURPRISED BY THIS STORM.

Our focus as parents had been to invest time in building character in our boys. When the boys were still so young they could barely sit still, we set aside time each evening for family devotions. Those Bible studies featured individuals who walked in integrity. The real-life examples often included mistakes and wrong decisions, but ultimately their devotion to God triumphed.

Over the next several days, I watched as Matt spiraled downward into despair. I stood by helplessly, buried by my own disloyal thoughts that it would have been easier for him if he had died than to live with the knowledge that he had taken a man's life. I questioned my convictions, my role as a mother, my values, my beliefs. Was God the same God I had envisioned Him to be for these past 30 years?

Psalm 139 declares that God knew me before I was formed in my mother's womb. He knows my ending as well as my beginning, and He has a plan for my life. But these Scriptures no longer consoled me as I struggled to breathe. The days and nights lengthened; peace and rest eluded me. With unblinking eyes, I stared at the black sky dotted with stars. Above the moon was the Throne of God, I thought, but if He still reigned, He had surely forsaken me.

> O Lord, God of my salvation,
> I have cried out day and night before You.
> Let my prayer come before You;
> Incline Your ear to my cry.
> For my soul is full of troubles,
> And my life draws near to the grave.
> I am counted with those who go down to the pit;
> I am like a man who has no strength,
> Adrift among the dead,
> Like the slain who lie in the grave,
> Whom You remember no more,
> And who are cut off from Your hand.
> You had laid me in the lowest pit,

In darkness, in the depths,
Your wrath lies heavy upon me,
And You have afflicted me with all your waves.
—*Psalm 88*

For three days and three nights, I did not pray. I did not read my Bible. I did not want anything more to do with God. I just wanted to crawl under the covers and not ever face another day. As I stared out the window at the stars, I could only think, "*John is dead; Matt is going to prison.*" None of it made sense.

Matt's life, as we knew it, was over. The superstar achiever, the role-model citizen, the professional soccer player—his life was dead and gone. What good could possibly emerge from such a heap of ashes? And now I was about to be tested in a season of waiting that would challenge every bit of my ability to endure—my strength, my faith, my beliefs, and my vision of life itself. The tidal wave had hit, and I was fighting to survive.

CHAPTER SIX
CAUGHT IN THE UNDERTOW

The first experience I had of a strong undertow while swimming in the ocean is unforgettable. I was in high school, and a bunch of us were riding the waves. After a dizzying wipe-out, I was unable to regain my footing. I tried with all my might, but as helplessly as a twig adrift on the surface I was being pulled out to sea. If I hadn't received a hand from a friend, a strapping guy able to withstand the power of the water, I probably would have drowned. I never again underestimated the power or pull of the ocean. Since then, I have witnessed enough lifeguard runs on the beach to see firsthand what happens when unsuspecting tourists have not heeded the warnings of a strong undertow.

The interesting thing about an undertow at the shore is that it's always assisted by a wave that knocks a swimmer down and pulls him under the water. The undertow, if it is strong, drags the swimmer out into deeper water as the heavy breakers roll relentlessly overhead. Regaining one's footing becomes an ever greater strain, and attempts to swim directly back to shore against the current will soon exhaust the hapless person. Sounds a lot like life to me.

The first three days following the news about Matt, I said nothing to God except to ask, "Why have you forsaken me?" I had no desire to swim back to shore; I was drowning, and nothing could change that.

On the third day, my misery prompted John to ask, "Anne, are you praying?"

I responded with unyielding severity, "No, I'm not talking to God. He'll understand."

I was disappointed in God; I felt betrayed by Him. I couldn't understand how He allowed another tragedy to hit my home and, more appalling, the home of an innocent person. The multiple burdens of pain and responsibility were burying me—from the losses of my son and my mother to the daily care of my ill and grieving father, and now this latest tragedy, all within a short period of time. *Really, God?* I felt pummeled beyond repair and too weak to even try to get better.

However, my dispatch of God into a time-out wasn't working. It only left me feeling even more out of sorts. I was giving God the silent treatment, but it was hurting me. The silent treatment only works if the individual withdrawing from the relationship really does not need the other person, and I needed God. Without Him, I had no sense of security, no purpose, and no place of rest for my disconsolate thoughts. So my knee-jerk remedy just added to the burdens I was carrying in my heart.

Thus, on the third night, I sought God like a spoiled, frightened child. I gave Him an ultimatum. I sat in my bedroom, silently crying, and said, "Lord, I am going to open my Bible right now; and wherever my eyes land, you have to say something to me. I am drowning."

I am not one to set up tests of faith like this; and, in fact, I am a skeptic about such tactics. But I was desperate and reaching out of my self-imposed silence because anything was better than existing in nothingness. I needed the Lord to speak to me directly through His Word.

Months earlier, I had begun to say the words, "You will not let my foot slip," when I was praying to God. I did not know why those specific words had come to me, but it was habitual for me to have Scripture slip into my prayers. Believers know that God's Holy Spirit guides and gives appropriate words for prayer petitions. Hence, for months prior to this "test," I closed my prayer time by saying, "Lord, thank You that You won't let my foot slip."

On that night, in utter desperation to hear a specific word from God, I randomly opened my Bible, looked down, and began to read the first passages my eyes fell upon. It was Psalm 121:

> *I will lift up my eyes to the hills—*
> *From where does my help come?*
> *My help comes from the Lord,*
> *Who made heaven and earth,*
> **He will not let your foot slip—**
> *He who watches over you will not slumber...*

When my eyes met the words, "He will not let your foot slip," I felt the Lord open the doors of my locked heart and mind, and the floodgates of pent-up emotions poured out. God said to me, "Anne, I will not let you slip. No matter what you see and feel."

Those specific words to me were distinctly personal and intimate. This encounter with God was enough to send me back into the comfort of His faithful arms. That night, I wept hot tears of sorrow that were, for the first time in days, mingled with a sprinkling of hope. It was a breakthrough moment.

I slept well that night, and the next morning I put on my spiritual music and spent time alone with the Lord. It felt so good to be back in communication with Him. Supernatural healing takes place when we let go.

LIFE PRESERVER: "God is our refuge and strength, a very present help in time of trouble" (Psalm 46:1).

From the pit of sadness I declare that God always shows up, and right on time. It is His nature, but it requires total trust and reliance on Him. God is always in control.

However, that doesn't mean that everything will feel fine, and life will work out the way we want it to. On this side of heaven, the trauma may never make sense and may be impossible to rectify. It's the way-down-deep knowledge that whatever we are facing, a personal and loving God is working on our behalf from the spiritual realm with an eternal perspective.

I then entered one of the most trying periods of my life, a time of waiting. We were waiting for the statement of official charges against Matt. We were told this process could take a few months. I suppressed the reality that my youngest son was going to be criminally charged in a major offense. I figured I would deal with it when it happened.

John would broach the subject as he endeavored to prepare me for what lay ahead, but I would stop him. My behavior with my husband brought back visions of myself as a little girl with both hands over my ears in the school yard, responding to the taunts of a bully with the words, "I can't hear you." I was withdrawing again as my way of coping. I felt safest when the gateway to my mind and heart were locked tight.

> VOICE OF TRUTH: THINK ABOUT SOMEONE THAT YOU TRUST IMPLICITLY. WHAT HAVE THEY DONE TO EARN YOUR TRUST? MORE THAN LIKELY YOU WILL SAY THEY CAME THROUGH FOR YOU AND WERE THERE TO SUPPORT YOU IN SPITE OF WHAT WAS GOING ON IN YOUR LIFE. I WANT YOU TO RE-MEMBER AT THIS MOMENT THAT THERE IS NONE OTHER LIKE JESUS WHO WALKED THIS EARTH AND KNEW WHAT IT MEANT TO BE HURT, ABAN-DONED, CONDEMNED, AND MISUNDERSTOOD. ULTIMATELY HE EXPERIENCED DEATH FOR THE VERY PEOPLE WHO CONDEMNED HIM. HE IS THE ONE WHO IS ACTNG ON YOUR BEHALF TODAY IN THE MIDST OF YOUR DISAPPOINTMENT AND SORROW.

During this time, John was busy researching the details in order to be ready to post bail when the time arose. He knew the bail would be high, and he was anticipating a need for a lien on the house. However, the timeline of a few months turned out to be erroneous—just two weeks after the accident, three state troopers showed up at my house with a warrant for Matthew's arrest.

I was at home with only Alivia for company. I felt my stomach drop as 3-year-old Alivia welcomed the men with her wide-eyed smile and proceeded to follow them around the room—these friendly visitors who were looking for Uncle Matt. I was forced to play along so as not to alarm her. The men caught on quickly and were extremely sensitive to her presence as they talked to me. The strain of the troopers' visit intensified when my 85-year-old father came into the house to see if everything was OK. He had observed the three strange men dressed in suits. Ironically, I stood in the security of my home, feeling anything but secure. The shock and stress of that awkward and unexpected moment left an indelible picture forever etched in my mind and on my heart.

John was out of town, teaching at a police seminar. Matt was in Philadelphia, recuperating from his knee surgery at Anthony's house. If he had been home, the troopers would have had to handcuff him and arrest him. I still shudder to think of how that would have been—not only for Liv, but for me as a mother.

My eyes fastened on the manila envelope held by one of the troopers. The envelope held the news—the official charges. The results of the investigation. Had the trooper placed the envelope in my hands, I would have dropped it as if it were a live wire. I backed away from it; I told the men I didn't want to know what the official charges were. They could call my husband and explain them to him, I said.

I shoved my protective gate right to the closing point, so barely a speck of reality was visible. I would keep the manila envelope sealed for as long as possible. I could tell by the looks on the troopers' faces that the contents of the envelope were not good. I expected the statement inside to redefine Matthew as a person charged with a felony—a felon. As I fought the threats encircling my home and pressing against my heart, anger once again raged in my thoughts: *"My God, my God, why have you forsaken me?"*

Further complicating my emotional state were Dad and Alivia, both of them watching the troopers and me with inquisitive eyes. I silently pleaded with my father.

Dad, please go back to your apartment. You're making this worse. I am having to pretend I'm not under great strain for your sake. Please go back out and let me be.

It was easier to deceive Alivia. She would not perceive my behavior as pretentious. But my elderly father—unwell and recently widowed—had to watch his adult child under duress. So I had to pretend. I tried to act like this visit was "business as usual." I smiled. I exchanged small talk with the troopers as I explained to them that my husband was out of town. I even joked that we had thought we had more time—"so much for having an 'in,'" I said, in reference to John's status in law enforcement. "We had been told it would be months before Matt was formally charged."

My tone of hilarity fooled my granddaughter and had her smiling at the troopers, who seemed to be friends of Mom-Mom. In retrospect, I think my father's presence, which he intended to be protective, gave me the additional strength I needed to withstand the difficult situation at hand.

I asked the troopers if I could call my husband. They were professional, but also seemed very empathetic to my dilemma. As I waited for the call to go through, I watched them studying the photos on my "Wall of Fame." That is a specific wall in our home that is covered with prized action shots of the boys, beautifully framed photos of the boys' athletic highlights from high school to college to the pros. There were several shots of Matt during his glory days—a life that would never be the same. I sensed their sadness—perhaps they had kids and could relate to how they would feel in our position.

When I finally got through to my husband, I put him on the phone with one of the troopers. My husband told them he would bring Matt the following day to turn himself in. I reluctantly called Matt to prepare him for the news, and my husband promptly returned home to set the bail process in motion.

Later that evening I heard the charges for the first time: first-degree aggravated manslaughter. Matt could get up to 20 years. I was numb. *Why would the charges be set at the highest degree? This was a good kid with no police record.*

I sat in disbelief as John explained to me that the charges were due to Matt's high blood-alcohol concentration of .21 and the fact that he was going 100 miles per hour at the time of the accident. All of those details were stated in the dreaded manila envelope. The vehicle he had been driving was a Cadillac Escalade—fully equipped, including the black box that records speed on impact. In law enforcement, high speed accompanied by a high alcohol-content reading are known as aggravating factors that warrant the highest level of charges. I felt sick. How could one wrong decision—the decision to drink and drive—reverse all of the good that existed prior to that evening?

The next morning Matt turned himself in. The judge set bail at a quarter-million dollars. This was much higher than anticipated, and John had to find a new source of collateral. Our house didn't qualify under the formula used because we already had a number of equity loans on our house. I watched as he tackled a seemingly insurmountable number of bureaucratic requirements and red tape in order to ensure Matt's release that very same day. The successful accomplishment of these numerous and stringent tasks in the short span of an eight-hour day was my first practical evidence that God was showing us grace and mercy through this process. Matt was released that evening.

Matt immediately went back to Philly to continue his recuperation. Anthony had had the same operation a few years earlier, so he and his wife, Anne, felt equipped to care for Matt and encourage him along the way. I felt completely isolated; trying to find light in this very dark tunnel was an ongoing struggle for me.

The next day, as I was getting ready to leave my house and go pick up my granddaughter from school, I was jolted by a man peering in my front window. It was a news reporter. I hastily backed away and peeked outside from another window. I could see a news van at the edge of my driveway. Two more reporters were banging on the front door. I stood frozen. I called John, and he told me to stay inside until they left. I was virtually trapped inside my house for what seemed like hours.

When the reporters were unsuccessful in getting me to answer the door, they walked around my neighborhood, knocking on the neighbors' doors. Undoubtedly, they were asking them about my family for a sound bite. When it seemed safe at last, I hurried out my door and jumped into my car. I drove to my sister's workplace and broke down in tears. I learned later that they had gone to John's office at the sheriff's department and tried to solicit a statement from him.

> VOICE OF TRUTH: DON'T FOCUS ON THE IMMEN-
> SITY OF YOUR SITUATION, BUT ON THE IMMEN-
> SITY OF YOUR GOD. YOUR MAIN FOCUS NEEDS
> TO BE AVOIDING THE UNDERTOW AND STAYING
> AFLOAT. WHATEVER YOU NEED TO DO TO KEEP
> YOUR HEAD SAFELY ABOVE WATER, DO IT. DO
> NOT TRY TO SWIM AGAINST IT, BUT RATHER STAY
> STILL AND ALLOW GOD TO CARRY YOU.

In order to stay afloat, I kept thinking of the story in the Bible about Peter (Matthew 14:22-33). The terrified disciples saw the Lord walking on the surface of the water as He made His way toward their boat. Peter, however, was moved by the power of God at work; he jumped out of the boat and boldly walked toward Christ. He was fine as long as his eyes remained fixed on Jesus and not on his circumstances. But the minute he took his eyes off Christ and onto the wind and moving waters, he faltered and sank.

I had no choice but to consciously remember Peter's example to get through each day. Fierce and frightening circumstances swarmed around me like a swarm of bees around a hive. I found that on the days I kept my eyes focused on Christ—His works, His mercy, His compassion, and His great purpose—I could walk. On the days that I pondered my circumstances, I would begin to drown in despair.

It was the fight of my life—resisting the strong current that was pulling me down into despair, and resisting the tendency to try to swim back to shore when I could not rely on myself. The only way to get safely back was "to wait," which meant relying on my faith as my anchor and putting on "trust" and "surrender" as my life preservers.

> LIFE PRESERVER: "As a man thinks in his heart, so is he" (Proverbs 23:7).

While I knew in my mind what I had to do, it was not easy. These conscious decisions required a physical will to perform. I woke up every morning feeling the weight of sadness settle on my back like a heavy garment; placing one foot in front of the other was like wading through mud with shackles on my ankles. Feeling a deep emptiness in my heart, I quoted Scripture to get myself out of bed in the morning, then sat and did my devotional time, listened to spiritual music, and finally stood up to face my day. When I wholeheartedly completed this communion time with God, I was able to walk in His Spirit and feel Him holding me together.

I never gave up on the notion that there was a bigger purpose at work in this tragedy. I felt deep down in my heart, as certain as I was that something was wrong at the onset, I was certain that something significant was being accomplished because the whole thing didn't make any earthly sense. I intentionally reviewed in my head a zillion times God's love for me. Speaking aloud, I claimed, "I am a daughter of the King; everything that happens to me must pass through His hands and His will." I reread my journals, which recorded God's boundless gifts of grace, mercy, forgiveness, and love throughout the past three years of seemingly unending and unendurable pain. I saw how God had managed my grief, and my faith and trust in His plan were reaffirmed.

Several months after Matt's accident, a friend sent an e-mail to me—a message she typed above a message I had sent to her just nine days after the accident. As I scanned the old message from me, I was shocked to read what I had written: "Thank you for loving me and being with me through all my tragedies (and triumphs). I look forward to see the mighty work that is going to be done through this and trust me it will be mighty for eternity." I could not recall feeling that way at the time—so soon after the accident—and I had no recollection of ever writing those words. But my message—sent back to me unwittingly by my friend—confirmed what I knew to be true from my years of walking with God: that even when a wave hits, and even while drowning, I knew that Someone bigger than me had me in His grip. It was my firmly held conviction based on a long-established relationship with God.

There is amazing power in remembering what God has done in the past—it's not just about recollecting a story or nostalgically recalling a memory. The Old Testament is filled with stories of God's people erecting stone altars to show the importance of remembering (and never forgetting) for the sake of future generations. The memorials, whether stone altars or personal journals, remind us of God's faithfulness. They call to mind the deeds of the Lord. It is an intentional act of taking note—reflecting on what God has accomplished in His people through events that do not make sense, except that God was at work.

"*I remember the days of old; I meditate on all Your works; I muse on the work of Your hands*" (Psalm 143:5). Such remembrance is the art of pulling from the past all of God's work, His essence, and infusing that into our present and our future. The very act reconnects us to God and reminds us of His activity in our lives. It puts things into perspective. God's power and love are not confined; if His hands did that then, He will do it again. I made a concerted effort to remember and recall, to meditate and contemplate on all God's works.

Matthew decided to come home to finish recuperating. His mood was morose, but resigned. He started leaving notes around the house for me, with the verse Psalm 46:10: "Be still, and know that I am God." I found this message jotted on paper and on my cell phone as texts and voice mail. *Be still. How difficult that is.* I wanted to move—to run, to swim frantically, to respond, to fix, to control. Matthew had realized the futility of our human effort, and the need to "*[b]e still, and know that I am God.*"

I saw God at work mightily through these past three years; I knew Him on a deeper, more personal level; and I needed to "be still" and let Him do His work. He had never failed me before. I fought so intensely because

I didn't understand the unforeseen circumstances, but I knew I needed to trust God unconditionally. Trust is one of those words bandied about with superficial regard, but trust is an act of total surrender. Consider the example of how one sits down on a chair, having every confidence that the chair will hold and support him. Watch a person approach a chair with the intention of sitting in it. Did he examine the chair? Turn it over to check the stability of the legs? Did he question its structure or its reliability? Probably not. Probably he just sat down. This would be especially true if the chair were a favorite chair, used for a long time by the sitter for his comfort and repose. The chair had proven itself again and again. There would be no need to doubt its ability to hold and support him one more time. I needed to trust.

CHAPTER SEVEN

TREADING WATER

The accident happened on Saturday; I had to be back at school that Monday. I didn't know how I would face the students, who surely had heard about it. In our small town, news travels fast—and, as the saying goes, bad news even faster. This tragic story with its potential for lurid sensationalism would gain even greater attention because of the high visibility of our family. I would have gladly traded all our past successes for the anonymity that would have permitted us to fail without the public scrutiny.

I wondered how I would face my peers, the faculty. What they would think about me, a fellow educator, with yet another glaring failure among my children—and an act as egregious as taking the life of an innocent man? After traversing the tough road of grief for three years, I had come to terms with my own failures and with the incessant self-doubt as the result of losing my son to drugs. I came out of that tunnel reconciled in my mind to the truth that no family is exempt from the temptations of drugs and alcohol. Parents cannot inoculate their children against those risky behaviors and dangerous choices as they would against other illnesses.

My thinking had definitely evolved. In the wake of John's 10-year battle with addiction, I had become acquainted with the studies on chemical imbalances, mental illnesses, depression, and brain diseases that predispose some individuals for substance abuse. Countless families around the globe—even "good" families with loving, caring, and consistent parents—have been affected by the horrors of drug or alcohol abuse. John's death had changed me in so many ways and actually made me more useful in teaching and ministering to others. My broken heart gave greater impetus and motivation to reach young people before they made the choices that could derail their lives.

Just as I had begun to feel recovered and re-energized with a sense of purpose, we were hit with this incomprehensible catastrophe. Just as we had begun to turn John's life and death into a passage of meaning; just as we were moving on from grief and doubt; just as we were regaining face and a place in our community. We were now the parents of the villain—"that guy." The drunk driver. The killer. I imagined that people questioned who we really were as a family, and I could not explain it myself. I felt the incredible weight of two blatant failures on my back, and for the next 10 months—until Matt's appearance in court—I was occupied with the strenuous exercise of treading water to stay afloat.

Having to play out the whole scenario in the public eye was made far more painful and difficult by a section in our county's newspaper, called "Spout Off." In this section, people are encouraged to contribute anonymous comments. For years, the practice has generated newsprint devoted to gossip and slander, and over the years I had condemned the irresponsible and harmful nature of "Spout Off" in my own column. Many others in our community agreed with me: There were occasional letters of protest to the editor; those anonymous cranks were called "haters."

When the haters inevitably resorted to chattering about Matt and the accident in "Spout Off," my heart was squeezed ever harder by the cruelty. I refused to read the comments, but I heard about them because they were discussed in my presence by friends and family members enraged by the lies.

After taking a hiatus from the world following John's death, I had carefully planned my re-entry with the new abstinence program. The irony sickened me, as I faced the predicament of having to teach under the cloud of another disparate incident. To make the matter worse, the objective I was hired to teach to high-schoolers was the "3 R's": Respect, Responsibility, and Restraint. Was God trying to humiliate me? The credibility I had gained in John's tragedy now seemed a mockery in Matthew's tragedy.

The conflict caused mental anguish. I did all in my power not to let my spiritual guard down, but it was very hard work. I was treading water ferociously each day, all day long. I trudged into the trenches, fulfilled my obligations, put on a convincing front—and the exertion left me mentally and physically exhausted at the end of the day. However, it is my nature to act on what I know, so I had to approach each day doing just that. I would begin by reciting the facts: I KNOW you love me, God; I KNOW you are in total control of my life; I KNOW there has to be a greater purpose at work.

I would tell myself these things over and over, KNOWING the power of what our minds dwell on in affecting the body and soul. But there were many, many days that my heart was not buying into what my mind was trying to sell. I had to continue to plunge ahead, regardless of my emotions, and focus on the task at hand. I walked one step at a time, which became one hour at a time, which became one day at a time.

My assistant, Kelly, and I repeated the motions of each day like Bill Murray and company in the movie *Groundhog Day*. On the car ride to school and on the way back, we talked and cried over the horror of the situation; but when we entered the school building, we had our game faces on.

I relied on Kelly to shield me from the curious staff members, with their intrusive questions. Acting like my protective pit bull, she interrupted conversations that grew too lengthy or personal; but she could not protect me from the conspicuous looks, exchanged glances, and furtive whispers that followed me. My determination to carry on, however, for the sake of my students and my certain belief in the value of the message may have garnered a measure of respect. When I entered the classroom, I immediately went into teaching mode with pleasant enthusiasm. The result was a receptive attitude of understanding from teens and teachers alike. I received nods of affirmation, sensitive touches to my hand, and cards of encouragement dropped into my book bag.

Those gentle, and often surreptitious, expressions nourished my soul and helped keep me afloat. They let me know that others cared without invading my carefully laid—and necessary—boundaries. I cherished every card I received, every meal that was dropped off, and every supportive e-mail and text message.

When a tragedy occurs, it raises up fear of the unknown. Our faith is tested by what we do with fear, not whether or not we have fear. I had to face my fears each day, and it required all of my strength. For 10 straight months, I woke up several times each night, gasping for breath. With palpitating heart, I felt smothered by fear—fear for Matt, for his future, for the deceased man's family, for the dissolution of the hopes and dreams of my family, for my diminished self-worth as a parent, and on and on. I would then recite Scripture to rebuke the darkness that threatened me: *"Greater is He that is in me than he that is in the world"* (I John 4:4). Eventually, I would fall back to sleep.

LIFE PRESERVER: "Perfect love casts out fear" (I John 4:18).

Difficult circumstances require enormous amounts of courage—courage I lacked on my own. I pleaded, I searched, I wasted away—and I waited. Being insecure in my circumstances caused me to gain security through total trust and surrender. Total surrender is exactly where God wants us to be.

In retrospect, I know that I met God more deeply in the middle of the hard stuff. I did not feel God at work in the moment—but I know He is always at work. I had to rest on that—"leaning into it" one moment, one step, one day at a time. St. Augustine wrote, "Faith is to believe what you do not see; the reward of this faith is to see what you believe."

LIFE PRESERVER: "Because He Himself was tested by what He suffered, He is able to help those who are being tested" (Hebrews 2:18).

Matt's court date was set for January 7, 2010. While my confidence wavered erratically throughout the 10 months before sentencing day, I knew I was moving forward. I was experiencing God's peace in ways that couldn't be apprehended by the human eye. There were moments when I felt the manifestation of a living God carrying me.

It was vital to me that I seek the larger purpose. My years of walking with God and getting to know Him and His ways—knowledge and deep spiritual lessons gained through experience—inspired me to believe there was a plan at work, a bigger plan. In humility, I prayed, "Lord, allow us as a family to step up and carry this cross in a way that is pleasing to you and blesses others who may be hurting."

I believe this final step of "full surrender" to God's ultimate plan was the key that unlocked the spiritual possibilities and filled our hearts with peace and grace. It created the opportunities to see God's hand work in great and miraculous ways in the midst of terrible and regrettable tragedy. It sure beat hiding under the bed in fear and despair.

Several months after Matt's accident, he was approached by a group called the South Jersey Traffic Safety Alliance. The group invited him to an interview with law-enforcement officials, regarding the prospect of sharing his experience with high-school and college students. Ordinarily, the Alliance enlists victims of traffic accidents (or the family of victims) as public speakers in an effort to impact young people with the horrific consequences of drinking and driving.

The Alliance was intrigued by Matt's story because he was "that guy" in the community—well-known, goal-oriented, and successful. One bad decision had suddenly and irrevocably overturned his entire world and ended the life of an innocent man. Matt's interview went so well that the group decided to work with him in putting together a program to be used in high schools and colleges. The program, written and formatted by Matt, was entitled, "I'm That Guy," and the message was *don't be* "that guy" or "that girl." It highlighted Matt's life with all of its promise—and the end result of one fateful decision: a man dead, and Matt going to prison as punishment for the criminal act.

Matt's presentation was the first time the Alliance introduced the audience to the experience from the offender's perspective, instead of from the victim's point of view. No one was prepared for the astonishing response. The message was powerful; the students sat riveted in silence during each assembly. Following the program, Matt was bombarded with questions. His Facebook page blew up with personal messages from those who attended, relating to him on all levels. Matt was young; he was accomplished; he had a good family; he made a mistake; he was going to prison. His was not the face of a drunk driver, the face of a felon. It was their face, and they were getting the message—"I could be that guy."

I anxiously watched Matt during this time, praying fervently that he would find peace, reconcile his guilt, and rely on the fact that God was at work—accomplishing a greater purpose in spite of Matt's fatal decision. Each time he came home after presenting the program, it appeared that layers of torturous agony were being peeled off his shoulders. The program offered a redemptive factor for Matt, and I was grateful that he could do some good out of this mess. The calls to the Alliance for the program came from all over as word spread throughout the state. In just two short months, from October until the start of December, Matt spoke in 34 schools, reaching over 7,000 young people. A list of requests from schools went unfulfilled due to the shortage of time—January 7 was rapidly approaching.

Each member of our family exhibited different emotions during the long 10 months of waiting. The accident happened on March 7, 2009. He was officially charged on March 20, and he pled guilty to first-degree aggravated manslaughter on October 7. His sentencing date was January 7, 2010.

Waiting requires laborious effort. It is unnatural to wait. We are wired to move, to grab hold, to fix, to fight, to flee, to do whatever it takes to resolve the situation—especially on behalf of our loved ones. Waiting is not a comfortable position nor is it a normal stance. Waiting can suck the life out of a person. It is draining.

When I walked through grief, it was a process of adaptation to a new normal. It was accepting life without a cherished individual; it was learning to redesign and create new models of daily living in order to cope with a huge hole in my heart. That process is enough hard work for a lifetime.

This vacuum called "wait" was much different. Instead of a process, which suggests movement; instead of a sense of gaining inroads, I felt stuck—I was treading water. I had to watch my child suffer, and I was not able to do anything to make the pain better, to fix it or to take it away. I watched Matt gather up the important items from his life and place them away in a safe spot, knowing he would be gone for a number of years. I saw him give away most of his clothes to his friends and brothers. These were the little things that had the potential to sink me into an abyss of melancholy.

In May, our family went to Florida for what we knew would be our last time vacationing with Matt for a while. While my thoughts were never far from the family of Hort Kap, the man who had lost his life two months previously, I still mourned for the loss of Matt's life as it was; and I was troubled about the future that lay ahead for him. I grieved for the time he would be separated from us. And I shared his sorrow and pain over the lives he had altered.

In Florida, I got up early each day and went for a jog with my spiritual music blasting in my ears. I then read my daily devotional and studied Scripture, holding on to every word as a special message from God. One morning, as I sat by the pool, I pleaded with God to help me, to encourage me, to speak to my heart—the yearnings that were with me every minute of every day. As I looked up toward the sky, there were the words, "Jesus Loves You." A ministry of sky-writing was the means by which God reached me that day, as I had no doubt the message had been written just for me.

On another day, the Lord again visited me in the early morning as I sat by the pool with a cup of tea. A mother appeared, pushing her severely disabled son's wheelchair to the very edge of the pool. Lovingly, she rubbed the water onto his legs. It was obvious to me that she had deliberately chosen this hour of the day, when her son could enjoy the pool in quiet solitude. It was a revelation for me. My eyes were opened, and I was able to see the lesson the Lord was revealing: My son was alive and uninjured; he was healthy and whole. He was not disabled. (Matt's passenger, a friend named Mike, had also been spared any injuries.) Through the grace of God, these unexpected pictorials shifted my attitudes from negative to positive. God loved me. And there were others with heavier burdens than mine—such as the Kaps, who would never have their father return to them again.

I treasured this respite away from the familiar, but it was hard on Matt to see me upset. He was put off by my tears—reminders to him of his failure and its effects. He would watch me intensely when interacting with friends and family to ensure that I wasn't dwelling on him. I tried to encourage him with assurances that God was in control, there was a bigger purpose, and we would get through this even stronger. Secretly, I prayed continuously that time would stop and freeze or that it would fast-forward a number of years until we were through this difficult time. My daily devotional book took on the symbol of an hourglass in my mind, with each finished page a reminder that the sands of time were passing and the new year was approaching—sentencing day was just a heartbeat away.

The commencement of the school year and the subsequent return to teaching as well as the demand for "That Guy" presentations caused time to take flight in even greater measures—challenging my daily quest for peace. In mid-November, anxiety over the upcoming holidays as well as the approach of the anniversaries of John's death and Mom's death coupled with the looming day of sentencing, all combined to prompt a decision. The idea inserted itself in my mind like an arrow thrust into its target. Having just completed my time of prayer, I thought, "*Anne, you talk so much about the power in prayer; well, why not increase that power by asking others to join with you in specific requests?*"

I immediately felt peace, and I wrote the following letter. The petitions of my heart flowed across the paper. I gave the letter to my family, friends, church members, and Bible study groups. Unbeknownst to me, many of those people made copies of the letter and passed it to their networks. I am unaware of the final tally of individuals who lifted these requests to Heaven, but I know it was a multitude.

I wrote:

12/09
Dear Brothers and Sisters in Christ,
    As this advent season is upon us, our focus continues to be on the amazing gift of our Lord and Savior Jesus Christ, the Father of all mercies whose steadfast love endures forever. We, as a family, have felt His sustenance in amazing ways. The month of December will always hold

an extra-tender spot in our hearts, as it is also the time of year when our son John was called home to the Lord. Losing a child has a way of refocusing our time and attention from this life to things eternal. And that is good!

And so it is with this amazing knowledge of the grace of our Lord, that we humbly implore you to uphold our family in prayer specifically beginning on December 15th (anniversary of John's new home in heaven) through to January 7th, when our beloved son Matthew will be sentenced. We absolutely know that "God causes all things to work together for good to those that love Him and are called according to His purpose" (Romans 8:28). We claim that verse for our lives and give Him thanks in the midst of this trial, knowing that something far greater is at work here.

As a family, we believe in the power of prayer, and if you are getting this letter, we feel you are part of our spiritual family and would like to lay out some specific requests for you to place before the Throne on our behalf.

As Matt's mom, I want you to know that his name means "gift from God," and he has truly been a gift to us his entire life. When each of my children turned 12, I bestowed upon them a biblical role model and life verse that I felt the Lord had shown me through their own distinct personality and leanings. Our Matthew's surname was "Daniel," and each day for years I would specifically pray on Matt's behalf: "O Lord, may Matt be a Daniel to his generation and not bow down to the gods of this world. May he be steadfast and strong and bear up under any lion's-den tribulations that may be placed in his life."

His life verse is Proverbs 3:5-6, "Trust in the Lord with all of your heart and lean not on your own understanding. In all your ways acknowledge Him, and He will direct your path." With that in mind, please pray for Matt's future, his cell mates and prison guards, that he may grow in favor with God and men in supernatural ways.

Please pray for the Hort Kap family that they might be consoled and see Christ in the midst of their pain through our witness to them, and that they extend forgiveness to Matthew and see greater purpose to this tragedy.

And finally, please hold Judge Michael Donio and Prosecutor Ted Housel in special prayer as Matt's complete life profile has been placed in their hands. We know that the ultimate decision will rely on the Lord's will "who turns the hearts of men any which way He pleases" (Proverbs 16:9).

I am praying the same scenario as found in the book of Esther 6: "That night the king could not sleep. So he commanded them to bring the book of the records of the chronicles to be read to the king. In it was found written a plot against the king." The story goes on to show God's perfect timing in intervening for His people and how He works in the hearts of men. So my prayer: "May Judge Donio not be able to rest after reading the history of Matt's life, and may he be so troubled in soul and spirit that he feels compelled to exercise supernatural judgment, accompanied by mercy."

We thank you for your love, support, encouragement, and most importantly, want you to know that you have held and sustained us in amazing ways during these trying years. We are eternally grateful for your friendship, and rest in the knowledge that our God is good all of the time and that He does ALL things well.

The Maher Family

It was through the power of prayer that peace descended on my heart and on my spirit. The seismic storm we were caught in was about to be quelled by the mighty hand of God.

CHAPTER EIGHT
STORMPROOF

*O*ur last official family portrait was taken September, 2005, at the party for my husband's retirement as chief of police. I cherish this photograph—from left to right: Michael, Little John, Mary Kate, me, John, Anthony, Anne, and Matthew.

We all know that pictures can be deceiving. Faces can assume the poses of happiness, tranquility, and love even as the lives reflected in the freeze-frame of the moment are falling apart. But not this picture, and not this night. At that moment, everything was picture-perfect;

and I believe that evening, captured in this reminder photograph, was provided by God as a special farewell gift for us because three short months later Little John would die.

Months earlier, I organized the calendar like a circus ringmaster, trying to secure a date that would ensure the presence of all four boys. It was no easy feat accommodating everyone's busy schedules. Looking back, I am grateful that I insisted on finding that single block of time when each one could be present. This involved juggling one son's professional soccer schedule, another son's college soccer schedule, another son stationed in the military, and another son's work schedule.

The party's program filled the evening with formal presentations, and the time was passing quickly. More than once, I ran across the path of the photographer and hastily reminded him that I wanted a picture taken with my family. "You never know when we will all be together again," I said, recalling the difficulty in gathering my far-flung offspring—an accomplishment I came to see as an act of divine providence.

The party was attended by family and close friends, my husband's professional peers, dignitaries and politicians, and the young men who knew him as "Coach." It was an honor John deserved, and I relished the occasion to see him formally commended for his years of service to law enforcement, to the community, and to youth. Speaker after speaker told stories, ranging from the humorous to the serious. Anthony and Michael delivered their own moving speeches about Dad, highlighting John's commitment to his family and his unfaltering integrity. Throughout the evening, Little John, seated alongside Mary Kate, held their beautiful newborn daughter. He beamed at the fuss and attention they received. The elegant banquet hall shimmered and glowed in the enveloping air of love and appreciation.

When the party was over, the boys decided to continue the celebration with their friends at a local gathering spot. So rare was the opportunity to hang out together that they were reluctant to call an end to the night. Never did any one of them imagine it would be the last time they would go out as the "four Maher brothers."

Michael, John, Anthony, Matthew

After their brother John died, the boys told me an account of that night together—about how the four of them sat and discussed the awards, accolades, sentiments, and anecdotes shared by so many people about their father. Many of the stories told were new to them (and to me). As children, they really had not had an accurate picture of John's impact and influence within the community and particularly in his workplace. And as grown men, they had gone off to college and moved onto their own career paths. Also, their dad was not one to brag: He never tooted his own horn or brought home tales of his successes. John much preferred to hear about his children's lives and their exploits. So this night of revelations moved their hearts in new ways.

Anthony, Michael, and Matthew told me that they were sharing how surprised they were, when Little John spoke up very matter-of-factly and said, "I'm not surprised at all; that's our dad." After their brother's death, the boys shared John's words of admiration with their father; and it brought him comfort.

> LIFE PRESERVER: "Death and life are in the power of the tongue" (Proverbs 18:21).

That once proud family portrait, hanging on the wall of my living room, now caused my stomach to dip with sadness. I cherished that portrait after John's death, but it became a great source of pain after Matt's accident. Whenever this picture caught my eye, my mind honed in on the invisible cracks running through the center. The portrait represented nothing but a reminder of a family shattered. I saw nothing more than the heartache of a son who was no more and a son whose life would be no more. That special night had become a façade, and I questioned what was real and reliable. That perfect night, full of hope and promise for the future, had vanished like mist. When I gathered my brood together for that family portrait, the storms were already taking shape on the horizon.

One thing is certain: The portrait is a constant reminder that nothing lasts forever here on earth. I know that life can change in a moment, and sometimes what you see on the surface is very different from what is happening below the surface.

Encounters with the storms have changed me. They have beaten me down, tossed me around, tested me, but ultimately I have come to the realization that they have weathered me and made me stronger. God's plan for my life involved a much different path than I would have ever chosen. I needed to surrender and accept His good and perfect plan for my life—every lousy piece of it.

Christmas 2010 came and went and before I knew it, the dreaded week of Matt's sentencing was upon us. My daily devotions seemed to be screaming messages on the importance of trust and surrender. And, like a drowning victim, I had no other choice at the moment of truth but to trust and surrender—completely and totally. Strangely, I began to feel with every part of my being that I was becoming stronger. I know I consciously and deliberately resigned myself that God would perfect His divine will on my life, and it would be for my own good no matter what that looked like or felt like. Because of the mental exercise of standing on God's promises, my fears began to subside substantially. I remember someone telling me that drowning is the most peaceful way to die once the fight for life stops. Ironically, I stopped struggling to maintain what was lost, and I simply let go—only to discover that I did not sink, but was held up by God.

The day before sentencing, January 6, was also the first anniversary of my mother's death. Matt asked his grandfather, his aunt Denise ("Aunt Dee"), his friend Alex, and me to join him at his favorite local restaurant for lunch. He wanted to make this a special day for Grandpop, and he instructed me, "No tears, Mom."

I felt from the beginning that Matt was actually looking forward to his sentencing day with more than a "get it over with" attitude, but sincerely from the point of seeking redemption. I believe he wanted to accept punishment in hopes that it would somehow make him feel better about the tragedy he caused.

I believe this lunch was a precursor of the extraordinary grace that comes to God's children when they tell Him they can't do it and rely on Him to do it for them. In spite of the heaviness of the day—the anniversary of my mom's death and the scheduled sentencing of my youngest son to prison the very next day—I felt oddly at peace. We enjoyed a wonderful time, and any onlooker would never have imagined by our conversation and laughter the weighty matters that were upon our shoulders at that moment. How could this be possible? I don't know in human terms, but I do know that the decisive act of "surrender and trust" pours grace out like rain—and we had a downpour for those few exceptional hours.

Later that day, our house gradually filled as friends and family began arriving to say their final "good-byes" before Matt's sentencing. I felt torn by the scene. The compassionate displays were reminiscent of John's death, when crowds flooded our home, bearing food and offering solace. Deep down, I couldn't wait for everyone to leave. Their lingering presence put me on edge.

I patiently longed for our house to empty so we could gather together for some quiet time and go over the next day's proceedings. I also wanted to do a Bible study and have a time of prayer. When the last person finally left, we took our seats; I opened the Bible and read from 2 Samuel 12:11-23—a passage regarding fasting and praying and God's judgment. We had fasted and prayed; and we knew that whatever the outcome of the next day, it was purely in God's hands for His final judgment. We prayed together, asking the Lord for favor and grace. I kissed and hugged Matt, then went up to bed with the most profound resignation of spirit I had ever experienced.

Early the next morning, I lifted my head from a pillow wet with tears and reached for my Bible and devotion books. I had chosen to rise early so I could spend some quiet time before getting ready for court. My devotion time further fueled the inexplicable peace that had entered my spirit and calmed any remaining uncertainties for the unthinkable day that lay ahead. I was thankful, and I felt fully assured that God was holding me and speaking to me.

What were the chances that on this very morning the Scripture verses in my devotional would be Matt's very own life verses: "Trust in the Lord with all of your heart, and lean not on your own understanding; in all your ways acknowledge Him, and He shall direct your paths" (Proverbs 3: 5-6)? Beginning my day with that specific reminder was personal enough to feel God giving me a big hug from the heavens.

LIFE PRESERVER: "For the Word of God is living and powerful, and sharper than any two-edged sword, piercing even to the division of soul and spirit, and of joints and marrow, and is a discerner of the thoughts and intents of the heart" (Hebrews 4:12).

A devotional book that I was consuming as if it were my breakfast was *Pathways to His Presence*, by Dr. Charles Stanley. The following words were my sustenance that morning as my eyes feasted on them. As I sat alone in my room on the day my youngest son would appear in court and be sentenced to prison, I read:

God knows far more about your future than you ever could. He allows roadblocks so you will not be diverted from His best. Instead of giving in to self-pity, consider why God has prevented you from continuing. You will come to a deeper understanding of how He heals, protects, and directs you. And you will learn that He is truly trustworthy.

The devotional prayer was: "Lord, it is hard to trust before I understand. But you know all, and I bow to Your knowledge of what is best for my life, in good times and bad." Amen.

I paused in awe of how personal God was for me at that very moment. Those words were my *life pre-servers*. Each and every one of them strengthened me in incalculable ways. As I would soon witness, this was just the beginning of watching how God could calm a storm.

I closed my books, got out of bed, and ran into Matt in the hallway. He asked, "How did you sleep?"

"Great. How 'bout you?"

"Great."

It was a surreal experience. We both seemed incredibly calm and emotionally strong. It was as though we were getting dressed to attend an important meeting that would actually bring a sense of relief. This was definitely not how I had envisioned feeling on the morning of my son's sentencing to prison.

It was also not the way I envisioned my ride home from court. The following is a portion of the letter that I wrote to all of our praying friends after Matt's sentencing. The ebullience of the words best describes the court experience.

Dear brothers and sisters in Christ,

I am writing this letter so that I may recap some of the most amazing sweetness of God's love and favor that took place before our very eyes and hearts in court January 7th, 2010.

The evening prior to court, we had a short, family devotion time, looking at the story in 2 Samuel 12:13-23. I told Matthew that when Judge Donio rendered his decision, we would wipe away our tears and walk in it as the perfect will of our God and Savior. We prayed together as a family, reviewed our speeches for the following day, said our good-byes (without tears as per Matt's request).

I retired to my room and wept and prayed for two hours. And then I believe the angels put pixie dust in my eyes and I slept like a baby until morning. I awoke Thursday morning strangely invigorated and at peace, no fear or dread in my heart, neither any trepidation for the matters we were about to face. I think in Scripture that would be called, "the peace that surpasses all understanding" (Philippians 4:7).

So where do I begin? This was the most supernatural experience of my life. [...] As you know, I had sent out a prayer letter to all of our church family, friends and relatives outlining a list of prayer requests to be said collectively surrounding the case. Literally every request written in that letter came to pass and much, much more!

The judge is known to be one of the strictest judges in Atlantic County—which, by the way, is also one of the most stringent counties in meting out justice due to a 40-percent higher drunk-driving problem than all the other counties.

Obviously, through these 10 months, those facts weighed on me like a ball and chain attached to my foot, and I was wading through mud each day. This period was the heaviest weight I had ever endured. It was much different from dealing with the death of my son, when we immediately plunged into a process of grief and managing the finality of it each day.

This season was torturous because it forced us into a "holding pattern"; and the "waiting" was painful, like anticipating the fall of a gauntlet on your child's head, accompanied by the pain of looking into your son's eyes and seeing pain, disappointment, and sorrow reflected back at you.

I will say that through these trying 10 months, Matt has amazed me in every way possible. His mantra was, "Be still and know that I am God." He stepped up to the plate with deep remorse, and did all the right things to accept ownership of this awful mistake.

God showed immense favor as he was contacted by the Traffic Safety Association and in just a few short months had spoken to over 7,000 students with tons more requests all the way up to North Jersey (both college and high school).

The "I'm That Guy" presentation got so much press and so much feedback from kids that, for me, it was God making purpose out of this whole dreadful tragedy. And I could see it visibly healing some of the burden that Matt was shouldering.

[...] I had for months envisioned coming home from court and crawling into bed, de-

pressed and incapacitated. It was the complete opposite. God's amazing grace was so evident in the courtroom. [...]

So as succinct as possible here are the highlights: The judge really took the time and researched Matt's entire life. He read every letter [testimonials sent on Matt's behalf] and viewed the DVD of Matt's assemblies. He spoke so highly of Matt and said he believed that the night of March 7th was a "bleep" on the radar screen in Matt's otherwise amazing life. He called the decision an "apparition."

The judge said this case kept him awake, and that in the course of one hour life had changed for everyone. He used words like two families' lives "intertwined for a bigger purpose." He said that Hort Kap's life was now saving lives due to the program.

He read a letter from a student, who wrote that after Matt's talk he went out and got picked up by some friends. After realizing the driver's breath smelled of alcohol, he and a friend asked to be taken home. Later that night, that car would wrap around a tree and the back seat would be demolished. The young man wrote, "Mr. Maher saved my life." The judge wisely corrected, "Mr. Hort Kap saved his life."

I was humbled and proud to watch Matt's brothers speak on his behalf, along with traffic safety representatives, and the final plea by my husband. I felt the Lord's anointing on their powerful testimonies.

Then the most amazing aspect of all: After what appeared to be an angry outburst by the deceased man's son, the young man turned around in a split-second change of demeanor and offered his hand of forgiveness to Matt—and the hug. The entire court let out a collective sob. Twice, the judge appeared to be fighting tears.

The daughter of Hort Kap, Samoly, turned from the judge during her statement to where I was sitting and said, "I am the only Christian in my family, but now I have lost my faith because of this." We were all devastated by that statement.

I had previously requested a meeting with the family after sentencing, and they had agreed. [...] So after sentencing, we were all escorted into a room, and I poured out 10 months of emotion and sorrow. [...]

And then my husband said to Somaly, "Hate my son, but don't turn your back on God." You could see the Spirit of the Lord in this room, as we began to talk and share our sorrow and emotions and all the pain. We talked about being acquainted with grief, and we were able to relate because of our own loss. And then we asked if our pastor could pray.

They requested we hold hands. And there we were in this room, the Hort Kap family and the Maher family, holding hands and praying. Then we all hugged and cried and hugged ... My boys and I took their e-mail addresses, cell numbers, etc., and we have already been in touch and plan to meet. We all left together walking in the parking lot, hugging again. I told them I felt strongly that the Lord has put us all together for a bigger purpose.

Matt received a sentence of five-and-a-half years

at 85 percent (he has to serve at least 85 percent of the sentence imposed before becoming eligible for release), to be served in a State prison.

I hadn't realized how afraid I had been of the future until I felt hope surge again in that courtroom. And hope did surge. There was no way I could leave that court room after so vividly observing God act on Matt's behalf and then return home only to begin a new trail of worry about how Matt would fare in prison. That would have been a slap in God's face; it would have been dishonoring.

I had perfect peace from that moment on; I knew that Matt was fine and that God was going to prison with him. I never lost a night of sleep over Matt in his new residence; when my mind did begin to wander, I would remember everything the Lord had done to sustain us.

LIFE PRESERVER: "If I make my bed in hell, behold, You are there" (Psalm 139:8).

For the first time in months, I had something I could wrap my mind around—and it was the faithfulness of my God. The entire horrific experience had transformed me, from the innermost part of my being.

When John died, it took me a number of years before I felt ready to re-engage fully in the activities of daily life. Just two weeks after Matt's sentencing, my husband and I were asked to give our testimonies at two separate churches; and in God's grace, we did so unashamedly. It is the desire of the enemy of our soul, Satan, that we stay paralyzed in pain, grief, and shame; but it is the act of getting up and resuming the journey—particularly the act of speaking words of encouragement to others—that demonstrates the victory won through Jesus. And Jesus sustains us.

I will never forget the heartwarming and prophetic introduction we received from Pastor Wesley Newell of the First Assembly of God Church, Cape May. He said, "There is such a thing called Post-Traumatic Stress Disorder, which is debilitating to a person. Then there is such a thing as Post-Traumatic Spiritual Growth, and that is what happens when Christians rely on God in the midst of their storms, and that is what the Maher family will share with us today."

Pastor Newell's words resonated in my heart because I realized how much stronger we had become since the death of John, and the strength came only from seeing God's hand in our lives through those tough years. While it had taken me one full year before I returned to writing "Family Matters" after John's death, I wrote a column just three months after Matt's accident, which shows the spiritual muscle I had developed through that time.

There were many people, including the publisher's wife, who encouraged me to keep writing after the death of John—but who thought after Matt's tragedy that I would never write again. Many felt, as I initially did, that my family was totally shipwrecked and to remain in the public eye would be the last thing any sane person would want to do. But three short months after the accident, I was surprised by the Lord's prompting to write openly and transparently once again. I hoped to minister to those who were hiding in their own house of fear. One truth that had become abundantly clear to me is that faith is tested by what we do with our fear, not whether or not we have fear. [Column below]

THE GREAT SADNESS
(published June 9, 2009)

"The Great Sadness had draped itself around
Mack's shoulders like some invisible but almost
tangibly heavy quilt. The weight of its presence
dulled his eyes and stooped his shoulders. Even
his efforts to shake it off were exhausting, as
if his arms were sewn into its bleak folds of
despair and he had somehow become part of
it. He ate, worked, loved, dreamed, and played
in this garment of heaviness, weighed down as
if he were wearing a leaden bathrobe—trudging daily through the murky despondency that
sucked the color out of everything." (Wm. Paul
Young, The Shack)

When I recently ran into a friend, she sadly
exclaimed with tear-filled eyes, "How much more can
one family take?" I have to admit I have asked God
the same question. In the past three-and-a-half years, I
have buried my eldest son, my mother, and now I have
laid to rest my dreams for my youngest son, whose
promising life has been derailed by the fatal error of
drinking and driving. This action caused a tragic accident that took the life of an innocent man. The Great
Sadness descended upon my entire family.

I found myself uttering Christ's words to his own
Father, "My God, my God, why have You forsaken me?"
I wrestled with God, feeling desolate and abandoned. It
was all too much to bear.

My despair became obvious to my husband, who
implored, "Anne, are you praying?" I replied, "I'm not
talking to God right now; He'll understand." I know

through past experiences that God is strong enough to be dissed by me. Regardless of where I stand emotionally, God lovingly and patiently ministers to my heart until I find my way back to Him.

Again and again, I heard His Word in my mind: "He will not let my foot slip" (Psalm 121). I may let go or loosen my grasp, but God never will. So I was eventually able to repeat other words of Christ, the hardest words of all: "Not my will, but yours be done" (Luke 22:42). Jesus said this to the Father in the Garden of Gethsemane after struggling so violently and passionately to accept what He was facing: rejection and death on a cross.

From the moment I rested on those words, The Great Sadness began to lift and I embraced a greater purpose to all the pain. Instead of asking "Why?", the question became "What?"

When you are unexpectedly knocked off your feet and blood ruptures from your heart, and you are squeezed emotionally from all sides, it is an opportunity for great seeds of compassion to be born. It is then that God does His best work and uses tragic circumstances for His good purposes. There are some graces that can only be exposed in life through the fires of trials.

After years of teaching Sunday School, I have once again been given an opportunity to live the very words I teach each week. I pray for the grace to reflect what "walking by faith" really looks like. I realize that to live and grieve with hope looks much different from coping without hope.

I have gained perspective in that there are many others touched by far greater sorrows in their lives. I have found joy in praising God for the bad as well as the good because He is at work through all of it. I practice daily to walk in the spiritual realm, with my eyes on Christ, because to stay in the physical will only make me see the storm—and I will falter. I have learned that we as a family are very strong, and we will use all of our experiences for the good of others.

I am committed to confidently saying to those with "The Great Sadness"—whatever it may be—that God loves and understands each one of us, and He is waiting for you to allow Him to not only bear your pain but to use it. And I know firsthand that He wants us to remove the garment of heaviness and replace it with a spirit of praise.

I guess I would best describe my transformation as being stripped bare of all my pride and covered with a coat of grace weaved personally for me from my Father in heaven. My husband and I committed to use every bit of our pain, shame, and failure to point others to God and to encourage and lift up those who were trudging along their own road wrought with pain. How could we not? We had seen God's hand and been receivers of His miraculous deliverance as surely as Moses and the Israelites when they crossed the Red Sea.

After a lifetime of memorizing formulas, practicing rituals, and following rules, I finally understood the simple truth. What God requires of me is trust and surrender—no matter what the circumstances look like or feel like. When I accepted this truth and acted on it, I then saw the very hand of almighty, awesome, all-powerful and all-loving God standing right by my side. He had been there all the time. The sooner I let go and relied on Him, the sooner I could see His work.

LIFE PRESERVER: "Faith is the substance of things hoped for, the evidence of things not seen" (Hebrews 11:1).

It is the evidence of our faith—that which others will see through our own trials and tribulations—that embodies what faith really is. It is walking, when you can't see the path in front of you. It is hoping, when it appears all hope is lost. It is believing, when there is nothing left but a pile of ashes.

LIFE PRESERVER: "Your Word is a lamp to my feet and a light to my path" (Psalm 119:105).

I came to the realization that God had equipped me for this moment. I had spent my life being prepared for the undertaking without knowing the troubles involved in what it means to be called "God's people." Preparation for the difficult trials had been in the making years prior, as we sat down and taught our four little boys about God, in Whom we wanted them to trust. Didn't we teach them about Noah and the flood? David and Goliath? Abraham and Sarah? Or were those just fun little Bible stories, for surely God does not act on behalf of men and women today like He did back in ancient times?

Those four little boys grew and became men, and the best gift we could ever leave them on this earth is the value of seeing real faith—parents who loved and served God regardless of what the outcomes appeared to be.

> LIFE PRESERVER: "These all died in faith, not having received the promises, but having seen them afar off were assured of them, embraced them and confessed that they were strangers and pilgrims on earth" (Hebrews 11:13).

So I am left to believe that is our call today. While we may not understand all that comes our way in this life, we need to understand that it's not *just* about this life—but eternal life. I am sure that what we see down here on earth looks a whole lot different from the view up in heaven.

> LIFE PRESERVER: "'For My thoughts are not your thoughts, nor are your ways My ways,' says the Lord" (Isaiah 55: 8, 9).

I have come to the conclusion that whatever the Lord has given to us—from money and material blessings to our education and experiences—we are to use it all for eternal purposes because we are just pilgrims passing through this time on earth. If I can keep an eternal perspective, I can do this earthly walk with confidence even when I am in pain.

In the center of a personal tsunami, an individual can face it with godly confidence. I have learned to ask God to show Himself to me; to make my case to Him and share my feelings; then to walk by faith; listen by faith; watch by faith; wait by faith; and become intimately acquainted with God who loves me, who has prepared an eternal home for me, and who is working on my behalf to guide me safely there.

The Lord's plan for our lives includes different seasons, which may include times of "being still" or "waiting" or "persevering"; but all of those paths require the shoes of complete trust and surrender. It is important not to resist the Lord's plan through the storm.

The sooner I let go, the quicker the rescue mission will begin. It is the Lord's plan—I need to trust Him to carry it out, and then hold Him to that promise. There are no earthly elements that can keep Him from performing His heavenly task if we trust and surrender to His will.

"WAIT"

—Author Unknown

Desperately, helplessly, longingly I cried.
Quietly, patiently, lovingly God replied.
I pled and I wept for a clue to my fate.
And the Master so gently said, "Child, you must wait."
"Wait? You say, wait!" my indignant reply,
"Lord, I need answers, I need to know why!
Is your hand shortened or have you not heard?
By faith, I have asked and am claiming your Word.
My future and all to which I can relate
Hangs in the balance, and you tell me to WAIT?
I'm needing a 'yes' and a go-ahead sign
Or even a 'no' to which I can resign.
And, Lord, you promised that if we believe
We need but to ask, and we shall receive.
And, Lord, I've been asking, and this is my cry:
I'm weary of asking! I need a reply!"
Then quietly, softly, I learned of my fate
As my Master replied once again, "You must wait."
So I slumped in my chair defeated and taut,
And grumbled to God, "So I'm waiting for what?"
He seemed then to knell, and His eyes wept with mine,
And he tenderly said, "I could give you a sign.
I could shake the heavens, and darken the sun;
I could raise the dead and cause mountains to run.
All you seek, I could give, and pleased you would be;

You would have what you want—but you wouldn't
know Me.
You'd not know the depth of My love for each saint.
You'd not know the Power I give to the faint,
You'd not learn to see through the clouds of despair.
You'd not learn to trust just knowing I'm there.
You'd not know the joy of resting in Me
When darkness and silence were all you could see.
You'd never experience the fullness of love
As peace of My Spirit descends like a dove.
You'd not know that I give and I save (for a start);
You'd not know the depth of the beat of My heart;
The glow of My comfort late into the night;
The faith that I give when you walk without sight.
The depth that's beyond getting just what you asked
Of an infinite God who makes what you have LAST.
You'd never know, should your pain quickly flee,
What it means that 'My grace is sufficient for thee.'
Yes, your dreams for your loved one overnight would
come true.
But oh, the loss! If I lost what I'm doing in you.
So be silent, my child, and in time you will see
That the greatest gift is to get to know Me.
And though oft may my answers seem terribly late,
My most precious answer of all is still, "Wait."

CHAPTER NINE
LIFE PRESERVERS

When storms come upon you—and they will come upon you—you will need a life preserver to keep you afloat. Throughout the writing of this book, I have inserted *"life preservers"* along the way. Those scriptures, quotations, words of encouragement, and time-tested adages are intended to give you an assist, a glimmer of hope, a short respite or a momentary edge in resisting the onrush of waves coming at you.

I have always found it helpful to log my own personal "life preservers" in a variety of ways so that when I am doubting or full of fear or feeling hopeless, I can go back and retrieve them and allow them to hold me up. They also serve as reminders of how my faith has been sustained through time. I use them as stepping-stones that reveal a distinct path on which God has faithfully shown up at just the right time with just the right solution. Most importantly, I go back so that I might "remember" that my "God is bigger than any of my problems."

That one specific *life preserver*—"God is bigger than your problems"— came to me in one of my weakest moments, and in one of the most unexpected ways imaginable. It was during the vacation in Florida when we received the bad news that Little John had been arrested for selling drugs. I was trying to be as strong as possible in front of our friends and for the sake of my children. But my heart was heavily burdened, and there were things too complicated to share with everyone regarding the situation. My husband wanted me to keep everything under wraps until our vacation was over. He didn't want it to spoil anyone's time, neither did he want our other children to find out. So I put on a brave face, forced my emotions into lockdown, organized our boys, and chatted inanely with our friends as we proceeded with the plans of the day—which was to tackle the insanity of Disney's theme parks at Easter time.

Waiting in one of those endless lines, I started to lose it. My thoughts were out of control, as the multiple problems waiting for us back home in New Jersey careened about my head. Tears welled up behind my sunglasses and flowed down my face. Shielding my face from our group, I turned and found myself standing directly behind a large woman, whose T-shirt suddenly became a billboard with a message just for me: **"Don't tell God how big your problem is, tell your problem how big your God is."**

Those words refocused my thoughts on my God, who was indeed bigger than my problem. I wanted to grab that woman and hug her, but I wasn't keen on having park security show up to throw out the crazy lady who was hanging on to a perfect stranger and babbling about hearing directly from God through her T-shirt. So I prudently left the moment between God and me. I am sure that woman earned an extra crown in eternity for wearing the witness of that T-shirt. She may never know how she was used as an instrument of mercy and encouragement for a hurting mom that day.

So that is what I would like to do for you now. I would like to share a few concise words of wisdom written long ago by various people who have experienced their own storms and were brave enough to share the insights gained through them. The words are time-tested, and they have challenged my thinking and kept me afloat when the current was working doggedly to pull me under. I hope they bless you as they carry you through the waves you face. May they sustain you through your own personal trials, knowing the Word of the Lord is our living water.

First, I suggest an essential tool for keeping you storm-proof—personal journaling. Grab a notebook and begin to write. Write daily—even if it is only a few sentences. No one is checking your grammar or critiquing your emotions. This is your reality, and—in those hard times—it is your pain. You can trust God enough to tell him EVERTYHING you are thinking. He is your Advocate.

However, regardless of what you're thinking, don't rely on your feelings. Your feelings cannot be trusted. Your feelings will convince you that this is the worst thing possible and you will never recover. Your feelings will lead you to the lonely place of hopelessness. You must consciously exercise your reliance on God and His promises. You must repeat those promises from the Bible to yourself in spite of what you see and feel. Faith is not about "feelings"—it's about what is unseen. It's progressing down the steps, without the next step being visible. It's trusting that there is support, which is holding you and guiding you to the next step.

When John died, I had already been writing in a journal for a number of years. It began as a result of having a child who suddenly was walking off the path on which we had directed him and onto a path fraught with risks. I wanted to record prayers that would assist me in being a parent, when my parental control was out of control. It was my first experience with a wayward child; and the more he drifted away, the more I found ways to hold on to God's promises. I recorded those promises and claimed them for John.

This evolved into a journal (or diary), and I felt relief documenting my emotions and struggles with my son. There were many ups and downs during that season of my life, and it gave me great comfort to go back and reread some of my thoughts and prayers. It was especially reassuring to see how things worked out in the times of crisis. I could clearly see God's fingerprints on John's life—on all our lives—as He answered prayers in striking and undeniable ways.

During this time of journaling and intentional prayer, my relationship with God moved to an entirely new and different level. Because of John, I was thrust into a closer walk with God. I became more disciplined in prayer and more consistent in setting aside time for devotions (the study of God's Word). Without the traumas of John's defiance and addiction, I never would have known the deeper, more intimate bond with God. This time also revealed to me my very controlling and prideful heart as I resented how John was causing upheaval and embarrassment to our family through his behavior. The more I fostered a connection with God, the more I realized how many times I failed my Father in Heaven in so many ways and He never held it against me. It broadened my perception of my son when I positioned myself as a daughter of God who loved me in spite of my mistakes—and without resentment.

> VOICE OF TRUTH: AS HEARTBROKEN AS YOU MAY
> BE AT THIS MOMENT, CLAIM HIS PROMISE THAT
> HE WILL NEVER LEAVE YOU NOR FORSAKE YOU
> (HEBREWS 13:5) AND ALLOW HE WHO DOES ALL
> THINGS WELL (MARK 7:37) TO MOVE YOU FROM
> IMMOBILITY TO SPIRITUAL STABILITY—HE WILL
> NOT LET YOU DOWN! HE WILL HOLD YOU IN HIS
> RIGHTEOUS RIGHT HAND (ISAIAH 41:10) AND
> PLACE YOUR FEET ON A HIGHER PLANE (HABAK-
> KUK 3:19). OPERATIVE WORDS: TRUST, OBEY, AND
> SURRENDER. HE WILL DO THE REST.

After John died, I was able to look back in my journal at some of my written pleas and petitions to God on behalf of my son's life and struggles. In reading them verbatim, in the intensity of the moment that they were written, I became increasingly aware that I was continually crying out for *my* idea of God's intervention in John's life—which was PLEASE FIX IT, FIX HIM. After John's death, I could see how the Lord was hearing and responding in His ways, which are much "higher" than my ways (Isaiah 55:9). God was weaving His own tapestry from His heavenly perspective, which was distinctly different from my earthly perspective.

Oddly, the strange realization that the Lord was acting in mercy and compassion in freeing John from his struggles gave me great comfort. My child's death, as horrendous and gut-wrenching as it was, reflected an answer from a Father who heard my cries, responded to my prayers, and gave my child the best of all solutions when He took John home to live in peace for all eternity. My son was finally free of his pain. When I comprehended God in Heaven as a parent who perfectly loves His children (even as I imperfectly love mine), I understood that John was safely home. Having kept a journal helped me to look back and come to this difficult realization.

I knew it was important to force myself to write during those first days after John's death. As hard as it was to even think about sitting and expressing myself with pen and paper, I did it because I did not want to forget the details of the facts and the emotions—journaling had taught me the value of not forgetting. It was vital that I jot it all down while deep in the center of the storm. When the house was being lifted from the ground and the suction of the earth's force was catapulting it in a zillion different directions, I sat and I recorded what I felt. I wanted to remember, and I could not leave that to the unreliable service of my limited memory. Remembering is necessary as sustenance through the next cataclysmic experience of being *slammed*.

I gained such insight when I looked back and saw that every aspect of John's last hours rose like scaffolding—with each detail hinging on the one that came before. A slight variation would have changed the outcome. That did not discourage me, but actually encouraged me: I saw that the day of John's death was written before the foundations of the world—as was his birth. Psalm 139:16 declares, "Your eyes saw my substance, being yet unformed. And in your book, they all were written, the days fashioned for me, when as yet there were none of them."

Nothing I could have said or done would have changed a thing. I gained comfort from that. It helped keep me from getting caught up in the "what ifs" that can weigh a person down. It had already been settled in Heaven for some greater purpose, so instead of saying, "Why," I now say, "What."

So with the hope of helping you, here are several *life preservers* lovingly sent from me to you with the heartfelt prayer that they will be tossed out again and again to those who are drowning. Make yourself a nice hot cup of tea or coffee, and wrap yourself in these words of wisdom that have sprung forth in a timeless testimony from the grit of those who know God and have leaned on Him in troubled times. May they bless you and give you a godly perspective for your life.

LIFE PRESERVERS

"The beginning of anxiety is the end of faith, and the beginning of true faith is the end of anxiety."—George Mueller

"In the greatest difficulties, in the heaviest trials, in the deepest poverty and necessities, He has never failed me; but because I was enabled by His grace to trust Him He has always appeared for my help. I delight in speaking well of His name."—George Mueller

"Thou, O Lord canst transform my thorn into a flower. And I want my thorn transformed into a flower. Job got the sunshine after the rain, but has the rain been all waste? Job wants to know, I want to know, if the shower had nothing to do with the shining. And Thou canst tell me—Thy cross can tell me. Thou hast crowned Thy sorrow. Be this my crown, O Lord. I only triumph in Thee when I have learned the radiance of the rain."—George Matheson

"Dost thou wonder why thou art passing through some special sorrow? Wait till ten years are passed, and thou wilt find many others afflicted as thou art. Thou wilt tell them how thou hast suffered and has been comforted [...] and bless God for the discipline that stored thy life with such a fund of experience and helpfulness."—Mrs. Charles E. Cowman

"Each of us may be sure that if God sends us on stony paths He will provide us with strong shoes, and He will not send us out on any journey for which He does not equip us well."—Maclaren

"You have been in the storms and swept by the blasts. Have they left you broken, weary, beaten in the valley, or have they lifted you to the sunlit summits of a richer, deeper, more abiding manhood and womanhood? Have they left you with more sympathy with the storm-swept and the battle-scarred?"—Mrs. Charles E. Cowman

"Let us sing even when we do not feel like it, for thus we may give wings to leaden feet and turn weariness into strength."—J.H. Jowett

"My dear child, are you wondering at the sequence of trials in your life? Behold that vineyard and learn of it. The gardener ceases to prune, to trim, to harrow, or to pluck the ripe fruit only when he expects nothing more from the vine during that season. It is left to itself, because the season of fruit is past and further effort for the present would yield no profit. Comparative uselessness is the condition of freedom from suffering. Do you then wish me to cease pruning your life? Shall I leave you alone?"—Homera Homer-Dixon

"An active faith can give thanks for a promise, though it be not as yet performed; knowing that God's bonds are as good as ready money."—Matthew Henry

"Little faith will bring your souls to heaven, but great faith will bring heaven to your souls."—Charles Spurgeon

"Cease meddling with God's plans and will. You touch anything of His, and you mar the work. You may move the hands of a clock to suit you, but you do not change the time; so you may hurry the unfolding of God's will, but you harm and do not help the work. You can open a rosebud but you spoil the flower. Leave all to Him. Hands down. Thy will, not mine."—Stephen Merritt

"In fierce storms," said an old seaman, "we must do one thing; there is only one way: we must put the ship in a certain position and keep her there."

"This, Christian, is what you must do. Sometimes, like Paul, you can see neither sun nor stars, and no small tempest lies on you; and then you can do but one thing; there is only one way.

"Reason cannot help you; past experiences give you no light. Even prayer fetches no consolation. Only a single course is left. You must put your soul in one position and keep it there.

"You must stay upon the Lord; and come
what may—winds, waves, cross-seas, thunder,
lightning, frowning rocks, roaring breakers—
no matter what, you must lash yourself to the
helm, and hold fast your confidence in God's
faithfulness, His covenant engagement, His ev-
erlasting love in Christ Jesus."—Richard Fuller

"Everything that comes to us becomes a
chariot the moment we treat it as such; and,
on the other hand, even the smallest trial may
be a juggernaut car to crush us into misery or
despair if we consider it.

"It lies with each of us to choose which they
shall be. It all depends, not upon what these
events are, but upon how we take them. If we
lie down under them, and let them roll over
us and crush us, they become juggernaut cars,
but if we climb up into them, as into a car of
victory, and make them carry us triumphantly
onward and upward, they become the chariots
of God."—Hannah Whitall Smith

"Trials and hard places are needed to press us
forward, even as the furnace fires in the hold
of that mighty ship give force that moves the
piston, drives the engine, and propels that great
vessel across the sea in the face of the winds
and waves."—A.B. Simpson

"Blessed is any weight, however overwhelming,
which God has been so good as to fasten with
His own hand upon our shoulders."—F.W.
Faber

"The burden of suffering seems a tombstone hung about our necks, while in reality it is only the weight which is necessary to keep down the diver while he is hunting for pearls."—Richter

"Christ sometimes delays His help that He may try our faith and quicken our prayers. The boat may be covered with the waves, and He sleeps on; but He will wake up before it sinks. He sleeps, but He never oversleeps; and there are no 'too lates' with Him."—Alexander Maclaren

"To lie down in the time of grief, to be quiet under the stroke of adverse fortune, implies a great strength; but I know of something that implies a strength greater still: It is the power to work under a stroke; to have a great weight on your heart and still to run; to have a deep anguish in your spirit and still perform the daily task. It is a Christlike thing!"—George Matheson

"Are you in sorrow? Prayer can make your affliction sweet and strengthening. Are you in gladness? Prayer can add to your joy a celestial perfume. Are you in extreme danger from outward or inward enemies? Prayer can set at your right hand an angel whose touch could shatter a millstone into smaller dust than the flour it grinds, and whose glance could lay an army low. What will prayer do for you? I answer: All that God can do for you. 'Ask what I shall give thee.'"—Farrar

"I hear men praying everywhere for more faith, but when I listen to them carefully, and get at the real heart of their prayer, very often it is not more faith at all that they are wanting but a change from faith to sight.

"Faith says not, "I see that it is good for me, so God must have sent it," but, "God sent it, and so it must be good for me." "—Phillips Brooks

"Ice breaks many a branch, and so I see a great many persons bowed down and crushed by their afflictions. But now and then I meet one that sings in affliction, and then I thank God for my own sake as well as his. There is no such sweet singing as a song in the night. You recollect the story of the woman who, when her only child died, in rapture looking up, as with the face of an angel, said, "I give you joy, my darling."

"That single sentence has gone with me years and years down through my life, quickening and comforting me."—Henry Ward Beecher

"God did not take away Paul's thorn; He did better—He mastered that thorn and made it Paul's servant. The ministry of thorns has often been a greater ministry to man than the minis-try of thrones."—Mrs. Charles E. Cowman

"A traveler visiting a logging area in the north-western United States watched with great inter-est as a lumberjack walking alongside a moun-tain stream periodically jagged his sharp hook into a log and separated it from the others. The traveler asked the logger what he was doing.

"Well, these logs may all look alike to you," the logger said, "but I recognize that some of them are quite different. The ones that I let pass are from trees that grow in a valley, where they are always protected from the storms. The grain on those logs is rather course. But the logs I pull aside come from high up in the mountains, where they are beaten by strong winds from the time they are quite small. This toughens the trees and gives them a fine grain. We save these for choice work. They are too good to be used for ordinary lumber." "—Greg Laurie

The testing, sorrow, tragedy, disappointment or utter defeat that you experience will interrupt your complacency and disrupt your life. It is my prayer that you will see the flower of faith spring up from these very showers. This poem expresses it best.

"When thou passes through the waters
Deep the waves may be and cold
But Jehovah is our refuge.
And His promise is our hold;
For the Lord Himself hath said it,
He, the faithful God and true,
"When thou comest to the waters
Thou shalt not go down, but THROUGH."

"Seas of sorrow, seas of trial,
Bitter anguish, fiercest pain,
Rolling surges of temptation
Sweeping over heart and brain—

They shall never overflow us
For we know His word is true;
All His waves and all His billows
He will lead us safely THROUGH.

"Threatening breakers of destruction,
Doubt's insidious undertow.
Shall not sink us, shall not drag us
Out to ocean depths of woe;
For His promise shall sustain us,
Praise the Lord, whose Word is true!
We shall not go down or under,
For He saith, "Thou passest THROUGH."

—Annie Johnson Flint

From the onset of Matt's residence in prison, I asked him to journal his thoughts and mail them home to me. I knew God would be speaking to him louder than ever before in his life, due to the sorrow in his heart and his isolation from the world. His writings evolved into a daily blog, which we posted on a Web site we developed to continue the "I'm That Guy" story with the hope of preventing other tragedies like the one Matt caused. The website, <www.themattmaherstory. com>, attracted over a half-million people worldwide. Subsequently, Matt was asked to write a monthly column for the *Cape May County Herald*, entitled "Prison Talk."

The following is taken from Matt's blog.

SORROW
What is the prerequisite to plumb the depths of your own soul? Sorrow! But only if handled in a godly manner. When you can get a hold on

*your sorrow and learn to understand 'him,' you
will begin to learn that 'he' is the plough necessary to uproot wrongly compacted soil and
emotions. Our souls become trodden down
over time and left hardened by the resources of
life—until an earthquake erupts, or a trial en-
ters, and tears up the land of our own making,
opening up canals and ravines that we never
knew existed because the earth of our being
was never lifted. For me, I was settled into the
dirt of complacency.*

*O, how we so need sorrow to better un-
derstand joy. O, how we need to learn how to
let sorrow's leaves fall gently on our intellect,
while raking away the twigs of pity and despair.
Those two can have nothing to do with godly
sorrow, for they will prolong the landscaping
process—always putting it off until tomorrow.*

*I've experienced more clarity in trailing sor-
row, following 'his' beaten path to more depth
and control over my emotions. I have even
found 'his' irrigation in my life to be the very
reason there is no more irritation in my life.
No longer struggling with releasing my will for
God's. No longer responding to life based on
the surface survey. Rather, resting assured that
God's resources and minerals are within for my
soul's purvey. God cannot properly warm me,
until I stop wrestling with sorrow's blanket.
His comfort wants to flood my soul's depths to
filling, not just sprinkle my feelings.*

**Commotion and shallow emotion
Stem from lack of inner devotion!**

*"For godly sorrow produces repentance
leading to salvation, not to be regretted; but*

the sorrow of the world produces death. For observe this very thing, that you sorrowed in a godly manner: What diligence it produced in you, what clearing of yourselves, what indignation, what fear, what vehement desire, what zeal, what vindication! In all things you proved yourselves to be clear in this matter" (II Corinthians 7:10, 11).

CHAPTER TEN
THE STORM'S AFTERMATH

*"And there are also many other things that
Jesus did, which if they were written one by
one, I suppose that even the world itself could
not contain the books that would be written"
(John 21:25).*

The above Scripture concludes John's gospel in the
Bible. It is very telling, in that even though the Bible
is the revealed Word of God, there are so "many other
things" left unrecorded—including the ripple effects in
the aftermath of Jesus' life. Those ripples were powerful
enough to sustain "His-story" throughout history.

Each one of us is on a different journey; and an
individual's pain cannot be weighed, measured or com-
pared to someone else's. Are there variations in the
magnitude of tragedy? Absolutely. I know a mother who
lost all three of her sons on the same day in a boating
accident. I know of another mother who lost her only
two daughters at the same moment in a tragic car crash.
I know of a dad who is dying of cancer, leaving behind
small children and a wife. A dear friend of mine and her
husband have rearranged their entire lives following a
fateful night in which their son, then 16, dove into a
pool and emerged a quadriplegic.

Consider the families affected by atrocities so shocking that they are recognizable to the nation, and possibly the world, by abbreviated tags: 9-11; Columbine; Virginia Tech; Aurora, Colorado; Sandy Hook; the Boston Marathon; and, sadly, many more. Whether the tragedy is private and known only to a few or public and part of the media headlines, the accompanying sensation of having been thrown to the bottom of the ocean in an abyss of despair is the same.

We all have our own tragic stories, and my own story may pale in the face of others' experiences. The knowledge that someone else, perhaps your next-door neighbor behind his closed door, has it much harder lends a reality check and much-needed perspective. It is good to remember that others have pain when one is tempted to descend into the pit of self-pity.

However, I will reiterate that pain is pain is pain. A broken heart, a dream destroyed, a goal unfulfilled—all may have a differing amount or degree of cracks, but it only takes one crack to make the walkway unsteady, tenuous, fearful, and dangerous.

My heart's desire is to offer encouragement to you, so that you can do this journey with greater peace and confidence. You are not alone, and this tragedy will only make you stronger. It is essential to allow God to carry the burden for you. You will find healing by being transparent about your pain and disappointment; and it helps to share the weight with a trusted friend when you feel ready to do so. Ultimately, as you feel the healing process take place, keep your mind and heart open to finding a bigger purpose in the pain so you can use it to help others. The heroes of this life are the ones who bear battle scars; they have survived the onslaught. They are the people I want to run to when I am *slammed*. One day, you may be the hero others can turn to in their time of pain.

My life definitely turned out completely differently than I ever dreamed it would. The outcomes did not match my input. Or did it? I have always desired to be used by God. I just never understood the price I might have to pay to really understand His heart—and allow Him to change mine to make it more like His.

From cover to cover, the Bible discloses that it is the pressures of pain and failure which truly mold our hearts. Years ago, I read a book titled *Hinds Feet on High Places*, by Hannah Hurnard. I enjoyed it thoroughly. However, 30 years and a few tidal waves later, I reread it with new eyes, a broken heart, and a changed mindset. I saw all that I had missed when I read the book as a naïve, young mommy wearing her own ideals of a perfect life as blinders.

The main theme of the book resonated so deep within my spirit. I identified with the main character, Much-Afraid, and her journey. Much-Afraid's desire to be near the Shepherd took her on a perilous and unpredictable trek over mountains and down into valleys. The allegorical tale realistically depicts a woman's search that brings her to the realization that in order to get to the high places, we must go low; that acceptance of God's will, demonstrated in our surrender, is the way to the high places. I now see how that makes perfect sense.

Observation of nature shows that through pressure, beauty and power develop. The rugged peaks of a mountain come about through the storms that pound the earth. Pruning makes trees stronger and more resistant to storm damage.

Anything of worth had to go through some difficult process to be most effective. Pressure and heat changed organic materials into oil, coal, and natural gas—sources of power for several generations of people. Pressure and heat formed the diamond crystals, which are then cut again and again to create the valuable, multi-faceted jewels. Grains, such as corn and wheat, must be crushed and ground into the flour that makes bread. Soil must be broken up at just the right time and temperature or it will be ruined for the whole season and unable to nurture seeds and plants. Pottery is created by throwing and twisting the clay, then firing it several times to remove impurities. Likewise, steel cannot be made without putting the various elements through the intense heat of the furnace.

I once read, "When God wants an oak He plants it on the moor where the storms will shake it and the rains will beat down upon it, and it is in the midnight battle with the elements that the oak wins its rugged fiber and becomes the king of the forest." Could it be that when God wants more power, more beauty, more strength, more usefulness, more production, and more purity in our lives He sends more pressure?

You may say, "I don't care about any of that—I want my spouse, my child, my peace, my health, my security, my life." I know firsthand that it is human nature to resist pressure of any sort, particularly if it hurts. We try to avoid it at all costs. However, we can put our hand up to the One who will hold us up. I choose to surrender. It is a painless action, but it *is* an action.

I choose to gain strength from those who have gone before me, like the apostle Paul. Imagine going through all of his experiences in one lifetime, and courageously continuing on in the faith. Numerous times he suffered physical beatings and deprivation: Five times he received 39 lashes, three times he was beaten with rods, and once he was stoned and left for dead. He was shipwrecked three times due to storms, and spent a night and a day in the open sea. His life was threatened by bandits, multifarious religious groups, government leaders, and dangerously flooded rivers that he had to cross. He went without basic necessities—sleep, food, water, warmth, and covering for his naked body. He was imprisoned several times, and for many years, for preaching the gospel. Secular sources report that Paul died as a martyr in Rome.

I choose to emulate the example of Mary, the mother of Jesus, who faced disappointment and heartache as she watched her Son scorned and crucified by the very people He sought to help. She was an unwed mother, and her pregnancy with the Christ Child actually threatened her life as Jewish law dictated stoning for women suspected of infidelity. Although Joseph married Mary, after a dream inspired by God, and thereby preserved her life and the life of Christ, she most likely lived her life with the whispered speculations that surrounded the origins of her Child. Shortly after Christ was born, she and Joseph fled for their lives to Egypt—to escape King Herod's murderous decree against all males under the age of 2, as the covetous king sought to circumvent the fulfillment of the prophesied Messiah. How Mary's heart must have sorrowed for the innocent babes whose lives were taken because of the birth of her Son.

When Jesus began His ministry, Mary's entire family was vilified by their religious community because of the challenges posed by Jesus. The Bible records two times when Mary may have been embarrassed and distressed because Jesus chose remaining to teach over returning with His family. I imagine her frustration as she patiently waited for her Son to become the promised Messiah. Like so many others, she may have been disappointed when no earthly kingship occurred, no change of rule from the oppressive Roman government. And then the worst-case scenario: torture and death on a cross. In her limited knowledge and understanding, how many times might she have uttered, "My God, my God, why have You forsaken me?"

During those three horrifying days after Jesus' crucifixion, Mary may have felt consumed by grief, paralyzed by fear, perplexed and confused by the seemingly dreadful ending. I am sure she cried out countless times in those hours before Jesus' resurrection, "My God, where are you?"

I have stated those words in the midst of my personal crises: *Why have You forsaken me, Lord?* Jesus uttered those very words while hanging on the cross. Earlier, Christ had pleaded with the Father: *"If it is Your will, take this cup away from Me"* (Luke 22:42). Death and anguish, pain and suffering, tragedy and failures—the key to rising above the traumas and reaching the high places in victory are the words Jesus added to His plea: "Not my will, but Yours, be done."

Can I say with full confidence that the God of Heaven will see me through? Yes. And He will see you through. The life we will live in this body and on this earth is temporary—it will pass away. The only things that matter for eternity are the things done for eternal reasons—heavenly reasons. So we must understand our storms from the perspective of Heaven—and understand that our Father in Heaven is with us throughout the entire storm. It is my daily prayer to accept the sufferings I experience as God's way of taking me to higher ground, to the "high places," and to accept the sufferings as God's way of showing His character to me so I can be His hands and feet and minister to someone else who has been broken and thrown into despair.

It is my hope to pass on hope—hope in the biblical sense, which has nothing to do with wishful thinking. Hope is spiritual confidence in God that is not rooted in our circumstances; it is rooted in Him.

I choose to hope in His good and perfect will because I can testify to you in this modern day and age that He shows up. He carries me. He is real in my life.

May God be your personal *life preserver* to sustain you through your storms. And may you one day pass on that hope to others who are drowning in their own circumstances.